UNDERSTANDING NORMAN MAILER

UNDERSTANDING CONTEMPORARY AMERICAN LITERATURE

Matthew J. Bruccoli, Founding Editor

Linda Wagner-Martin, Series Editor

UNDERSTANDING NORMAN MAILER

Maggie McKinley

The University of South Carolina Press

Published by the University of South Carolina Press
Columbia, South Carolina 29208

www.sc.edu/uscpress

Manufactured in the United States of America

26 25 24 23 22 21 20 19 18 17
10 9 8 7 6 5 4 3 2 1

Library of Congress Cataloging-in-Publication Data
can be found at http://catalog.loc.gov/.

ISBN 978-1-61117-805-0 (cloth)
ISBN 978-1-61117-806-7 (ebook)

This book was printed on recycled paper with
30 percent postconsumer waste content.

Thanks to all of my family and friends for their unwavering support. Special thanks go to Mike Lennon and everyone involved with the Mailer Society.

CONTENTS

SERIES EDITOR'S PREFACE

The Understanding Contemporary American Literature series was founded by the estimable Matthew J. Bruccoli (1931–2008), who envisioned these volumes as guides or companions for students as well as good nonacademic readers, a legacy that will continue as new volumes are developed to fill in gaps among the nearly one hundred series volumes published to date and to embrace a host of new writers only now making their marks on our literature.

As Professor Bruccoli explained in his preface to the volumes he edited, because much influential contemporary literature makes special demands, "the word understanding in the titles was chosen deliberately. Many willing readers lack an adequate understanding of how contemporary literature works; that is, of what the author is attempting to express and the means by which it is conveyed." Aimed at fostering this understanding of good literature and good writers, the criticism and analysis in the series provide instruction in how to read certain contemporary writers—explicating their material, language, structures, themes, and perspectives—and facilitate a more profitable experience of the works under discussion.

In the twenty-first century Professor Bruccoli's prescience gives us an avenue to publish expert critiques of significant contemporary American writing. The series continues to map the literary landscape and to provide both instruction and enjoyment. Future volumes will seek to introduce new voices alongside canonized favorites, to chronicle the changing literature of our times, and to remain, as Professor Bruccoli conceived, contemporary in the best sense of the word.

Linda Wagner-Martin, Series Editor

CHAPTER 1

Understanding Norman Mailer

One of Norman Mailer's favorite quotes was that offered by Nobel Prize–winning author André Gide: "Do not understand me too quickly."[1] Thus, there would seem to be a certain irony in penning a book titled *Understanding Norman Mailer,* for in both his life and his work, Mailer embodied Gide's remark, resisting any easy exegesis or conclusions. However, it is precisely *because* of his investment in dialectic, intellectual rigor, and occasional elusiveness that Mailer's body of work can reflect the true intent of this book.

Understanding Norman Mailer does not purport to reach an irrefutable "understanding" of the author or his work, but to recognize that the process of deriving meaning from literature is an ongoing project. Such a project requires coming to terms with the idea that the answers are less important, perhaps, than the questions. As Mailer himself stated, "It is worth remembering that in life, as in other mysteries, there are no answers, only questions, but part of the pleasure of intellection is to refine the question, or discover a new one."[2] Moreover, while the endeavor to understand Mailer may be asymptotic, approaching but never reaching an endpoint, any serious attempt to appreciate and comprehend his work is still undeniably instructive and revelatory, as his work illuminates many of the dark corners of both the individual psyche and contemporary American culture at large.

Life and Career: An Overview

As a renowned novelist, journalist, biographer, playwright, speaker, aspiring politician, filmmaker, and public intellectual, Norman Mailer can be deemed one of the central literary and cultural figures of twentieth-century America, and certainly one of the most prolific. Yet Mailer did not grow up envisioning a career as a writer. Born in 1923 in Long Branch, New Jersey, and raised in

Brooklyn, Mailer attended Harvard with the goal of becoming an engineer. His elective writing classes at Harvard captured his interest and shifted his focus, however, and while there, Mailer wrote approximately thirty short stories, a novella titled *A Calculus at Heaven,* and two novels—*A Transit To Narcissus* and *No Percentage.* While there were bumps in the road (one of his stories reduced his classmates to laughter—and it was not intended to be a comedy), he eventually earned the respect of both his writing professors and a few editors in the publishing world. In fact, *A Calculus at Heaven* was published in an anthology, *Cross-Section: A Collection of New American Writing,* in 1944. (*A Transit to Narcissus* would not be published until 1978, when it was released as a limited facsimile, and *No Percentage* has never been published.) Ultimately, though, it was his experience as an enlisted soldier stationed in the Pacific during World War II that provided him with material for his first major novel, *The Naked and the Dead,* which he published in 1948 at the age of twenty-five. The novel immediately became a commercial best seller and critical success, and the sudden fame it garnered made him the darling of the literary world. While the levels of public and critical admiration would shift and change over the ensuing decades, Mailer remained a renowned public figure throughout his lifetime, a status with which he himself would often grapple, as this lifelong celebrity intruded on but also informed his writing—something he addresses directly in works such as *The Armies of the Night* (1968) and *Marilyn* (1973).

After the success of *The Naked and the Dead,* Mailer continued to publish steadily until his death in 2007 at the age of eighty-four. Over the course of his expansive sixty-year career, Mailer published nearly forty original works of fiction and nonfiction, crossing a wide spectrum of style and genre, as well as numerous articles and essays for various well-known publications, including *Esquire, Commentary, Life, Playboy, Dissent,* and the *Village Voice,* the latter of which he also helped to found. From the 1950s through the 1970s, a period often seen as the height of Mailer's visibility and notoriety, his output was particularly impressive. In the 1960s alone, for example, he published two novels, a collection of short stories, two essay collections, and two full-length works of nonfiction, while also directing three experimental films and and adapting his novel *The Deer Park* into a play. He won the Pulitzer Prize twice: once in 1969 for *The Armies of the Night* (for which he also received the National Book Award), and again in 1980 for *The Executioner's Song.* In 2005, Mailer was honored with the Medal of Distinguished Contribution to Arts and Letters, a lifetime achievement award granted by the National Book Foundation.

In addition to his lifelong commitment to writing and his foray into film, Mailer also embraced the role of public intellectual. He frequently engaged in public debates (most notably with his right-wing counterpart, William F. Buckley), appeared on television shows, and gave various lectures covering a number of cultural and political topics. As a result, Mailer became a revered, if also contentious, public figure during the height of his career. The 1960s and 1970s saw the apex of Mailer's celebrity—during this time he participated in the 1967 march on the Pentagon to protest the war in Vietnam, and was arrested in the process (an experience that he covers in *The Armies of the Night*). He also made waves in the political sector by running for mayor of New York in the 1969 Democratic primary alongside fellow author and journalist Jimmy Breslin, and he maintained high levels of visibility in the literary world by not only publishing fiction and nonfiction, but also penning a regular column in *Esquire* titled "The Big Bite."

The 1960s were, in many ways, the height not only of Mailer's fame but also his infamy. For example, his mayoral campaign (which Mailer's authorized biographer Michael Lennon has called "the operative definition of quixotic") was hit by some bad press when Mailer was revealed to have berated some of his campaign staff, calling them "a bunch of spoiled pigs."[3] Though this was not the primary factor in Mailer's fourth-place finish out of five candidates (he was, after all, the underdog and a long shot in the race), it did contribute to the reputation he had begun to steadily acquire over the previous years as a bombastic, egotistical womanizer, a hot-headed, heavy-drinking individual always ready for a fight (a reputation sometimes deserved, albeit a reductive view of his character). Contributing to this was his tendency to incite the ire of the women's liberation movement with a variety of inflammatory comments, some intended to be facetious and others intended to be serious reflections of his own theories of gender, but nearly all of which deepened the rift between himself and the feminist movement. Drama surrounding Mailer's public life would not end here. In 1981, for instance, Mailer vouched for the parole request of convicted criminal Jack Abbott, with whom Mailer had corresponded while composing *The Executioner's Song*. Soon after being released, however, Abbott stabbed an innocent waiter at a restaurant in New York, and was summarily tried and convicted for manslaughter. Mailer was deeply disturbed by the tragedy and shaken by the fact that, as he indicated in a press conference, he had missed some "little warnings" about Abbott's difficulty rehabilitating.[4] Nevertheless, he continued to correspond with Abbott over the next few years, and was widely criticized for this ongoing association.

Moreover, for many years, Mailer's personal life was plagued with troubles that were also placed under a public microscope. Perhaps most famously, he stabbed his second wife, Adele Morales, after a party in their home in 1960.

Though Adele recovered and did not press charges, Mailer was assigned court-ordered psychiatric care at Bellevue Hospital in New York, and spent later years facing public scrutiny of the event. Around this time, Mailer also began to contend with some serious financial problems. By the end of the 1960s, he had been married four times (to Beatrice Silverman in 1944, Adele Morales in 1954, Jeanne Campbell in 1962, and Beverley Bentley in 1963) and these marriages had produced six children. He would marry and divorce once more (to Carol Stevens, with whom he also had a daughter), before wedding Norris Church Mailer in 1980, to whom he would remain married until his death. He and Norris then had another son, and Mailer officially adopted Norris's son from a previous marriage, bringing his brood to a total of nine children. During the 1960s and 1970s, the cost of raising such a large family and paying alimony to his ex-wives, coupled with the film projects into which he poured a significant amount of his own money at this time, resulted in some large debts. Thus, despite his literary output and various speaking engagements, Mailer remained financially strained for many years. However, his marriage to Norris ultimately survived and outlasted these rockier periods. In an interview conducted much later in his life, Mailer reflected on this time with some bemusement. "I'm now eighty, but some people still regard me as a wild man," he says. "Even at my peak, that was only five to ten percent of my nature. The rest was work."[5]

While the controversy that has swirled around his personal life has sometimes gotten in the way of an appreciation of his literature, many of Mailer's personal beliefs and experiences—his service in World War II, his spirituality (shaped but not dictated by his Jewish roots), his theories and anxieties about manhood, the celebrity and infamy that colored his worldview and his work—are so obviously infused into his fiction that certain elements of his autobiography cannot be ignored. There is a fine line between recognizing and ignoring "The Author," and it is important to acknowledge that Mailer puts much of himself into his work while avoiding the tendency to conflate the author with his protagonists or over-privilege the personal.

Despite personal and financial strife, after all, Mailer remained devoted to his creative life, constantly attempting to break new literary and philosophical ground and refusing to rest on the laurels of his early success or to work within one particular style or medium. In the 1980s and 1990s, he produced some of his weightiest and most heavily researched tomes, which range from a novel about ancient Egypt to a spy thriller centered on the activity of the CIA. His final novel, *The Castle in the Forest* (2007), which focuses on the childhood of Adolf Hitler as seen through the eyes of one of Satan's devils, landed on the *New York Times* best-seller list, demonstrating not only Mailer's lasting success but also his lifelong investment in engaging with difficult subject matter in unique ways.

Narrative Style and Literary Influence

The variety and innovation exhibited within Mailer's extensive literary canon has led Michael Johnson to call him a "genre maker"—an apt term when one considers that Mailer not only tackled a variety of writing styles, but also frequently combined elements of these variant genres to create his own unique stylistic hybrids.[6] For example, in *The Armies of the Night*, Mailer employs elements of autobiography, participatory journalism, and literary fiction to fashion his own adaptation of New Journalism. He continued to experiment with genre until the end of his career, penning everything from an in-depth study of Gary Gilmore (1979's *The Executioner's Song*) to an eight-hundred-page epic novel about ancient Egypt (1983's *Ancient Evenings*) to a hard-boiled campy crime thriller (1984's *Tough Guys Don't Dance*), among others. Philip Roth made note of Mailer's tendency to traverse various generic grounds in his essay "Writing American Fiction," in which Roth observes that, "however one suspects Mailer's style or his motives, one sympathizes with the impulse that leads him to want to be a critic, a reporter, a sociologist, a journalist, or even the Mayor of New York. For what is particularly tough about the times is writing about them, as a serious novelist or storyteller."[7]

Despite his impressive literary output, over the course of his career, Mailer spoke often of his unrealized "big novel"; in *Advertisements for Myself*, his 1959 compilation of excerpts, short stories, previously published essays, and new self-reflections and commentaries (the "advertisements"), Mailer reflects on this goal to write a book that would be "the longest ball ever to go up into the accelerated hurricane air of our American letters" (439). While many of his novels are literally "big," some exceeding one thousand pages, none of these, in Mailer's own view, became that particular work he had been reaching for throughout his career, and many of his future critics were quick to judge his later works against this goal.[8] Yet this should not be taken as evidence of a failure on Mailer's part; in fact, it might be seen as quite the opposite, for amid the various trials, stops, and starts on the journey to produce this "big novel," Mailer produced a bevy of works that captured the sentiments of America at various stages of the twentieth century, and part of his legacy is thus his ability to enrich our understanding of American culture and history.

While Mailer's own unique voice is evident from the start of his career, his writing does not exist in a vacuum. When it was first published, for instance, *The Naked and the Dead* invited immediate comparisons to Hemingway.

Some of these comparisons were a result of stylistic similarities (Mailer himself noted that Hemingway was a significant influence), but much also had to do with the two authors' similar concerns—masculinity, individualism, and courage in wartime, to name only a few. Hemingway was not Mailer's sole influence, however. Mailer himself readily named the authors and intellectuals who had a profound impact on him in his early career, including John Dos Passos, Leo Tolstoy, James T. Farrell, William Faulkner, D. H. Lawrence, Henry Miller, John Steinbeck, and Thomas Wolfe. One of the individuals Mailer most frequently cited as an influence, however, was writer and Marxist intellectual Jean Malaquais, whom he met just after publishing *The Naked and the Dead*. Mailer had asked Malaquais to translate the novel into French, and during the process the two became close, with Malaquais becoming a deeply influential mentor. Malaquais, Mailer said in 1964, is "the only man I know who can combine a powerfully dogmatic mind with the keenest sense of political nuance, and he has a formidable culture which seems to live in his veins and capillaries."[9] In fact, in his preface to Malaquais's novel *The Joker,* Mailer wrote that the author "had more influence upon my mind than anyone I ever knew."[10] Malaquais's influence is perhaps most evident in Mailer's second novel, *Barbary Shore* (which, somewhat ironically, Malaquais himself did not care for). As the years went on, this influence waned as Mailer's own philosophies began to diverge from those of his mentor, though the two remained close. They had a falling out in 1994 after Malaquais publicly accused Mailer of losing sight of his literary vision as a result of becoming a literary celebrity; however, they reconciled shortly before Malaquais's death in 1998, thus ultimately preserving a decades-long friendship.

Though Mailer is known for some of his more bitingly critical appraisals of the work of his contemporaries, he also held many of his fellow writers in high esteem, forming friendships with a number of authors and intellectuals that were mutually influential. He very much respected the work of playwright Lillian Hellman, poet Robert Lowell, literary and cultural critics Irving Howe, Diana Trilling, and Dwight McDonald (the latter of whom biographer Michael Lennon refers to as one of Mailer's "intellectual godfathers"), and fellow novelists James Baldwin, James Jones, and William Styron.[11] Mailer formed a particularly close, if somewhat turbulent, bond with both Jones and Styron, his friendships with them weathering criticism, bruised egos, and feuds. Mailer and Baldwin would go on to form an interesting relationship as well, characterized by shared respect but also fraught with some conflict: while Baldwin looked to Mailer as a literary mentor early on, he was also critical of Mailer's theories about blackness, particularly about black masculinity (outlined most famously in Mailer's *The White Negro*).[12] Additionally, Mailer sustained a complex relationship with William F. Buckley, founder of the conservative publication *National Review* and host of the television series *Firing Line*. Though they were at opposite ends of the political spectrum in many respects and engaged in highly publicized debates in the 1960s—Buckley representing the far right, Mailer the left—the two men formed what Kevin M. Schultz terms a "difficult friendship" that lasted decades. This was not only a result of their respect for each other's intellect, but also because they shared a similar investment in the intellectual life of America, and spoke out against the effects of mass media and corporate corruption. As Schultz points out, Mailer felt he and Buckley "were both prophetic voices, standing outside the mainstream, offering critiques from a higher moral plane . . . both asking America to live up to its better angels."[13]

While Mailer influenced and was influenced by these and other contemporaries, he nevertheless worked to shape and evolve his unique writing style. Many credit *Advertisements for Myself* as being the text in which Mailer truly began to exhibit a distinctive voice and perspective; in fact, Mailer himself admitted that "*Advertisements* was the first work I wrote with a style I could call my own."[14] In this work, Mailer claims he became more conscious of the rhythm of his own prose, and began to depart from the weighty influence of his predecessors. He also credits *Advertisements* with illuminating the intricacies and difficulties of perspective. "It was not until I struggled with *Advertisements for Myself* that I began to realize how curious it was to be working in the first person," he said later, referring to the perspective he'd attempted in works like *Barbary Shore* and *The Deer Park*. "It's highly unnatural, because 'I' adds up only about a third of the consciousness of any human being. . . . there is a part of the ego that is superior to ourselves—that person who observes us carefully even as we're doing bizarre things, that special persona, possessed of immaculate detachment."[15]

With this in mind, Mailer continued to hone his writing style throughout his career, often experimenting with different forms of perspective. For instance, in *The Armies of the Night,* Mailer diverges from the third-person omniscient and first-person perspectives he had also employed in his early fiction and nonfiction in order to try his hand at illeism, a style that allowed him to write about himself in the third person, and which became one of his signatures as a New Journalist in the 1960s and 1970s. While he admitted that this perspective felt "damned odd" as he was initially working on *Armies* and that he was "halfway into the book before [he] got used to it," he also notes, "by the time I was done, I missed this character of Norman Mailer so much that I brought him back for book after book."[16]

Totalitarianism, Existentialism, and Spirituality

As Mailer's style evolved over the course of his career, so did many of his philosophies and opinions; however, there were a number of themes with which Mailer remained preoccupied throughout his lifetime. For instance, over the course of his career, Mailer demonstrated a deep concern regarding the problem of totalitarianism, particularly its manifestation in American society. It was his belief that totalitarianism was not only a political and social threat enacted against the freedom of the individual, but that it had also made inroads into every aspect of society, from architecture to technology. As he wrote in *Commentary* in 1963, "The entrance of the Devil into aesthetics is visible in a new airline terminal, a luxury hotel, a housing project, or a civic center. Their flat surfaces speak of power without vision, their plastic materials suggest flesh without the unimaginable details of blood."[17] His skepticism about technology as a contributing factor to this kind of mind-numbing totalitarianism also remained one of his central concerns; in *On God*, a series of conversations with Michael Lennon published just before Mailer's death in 2007, he says that technology might be "the most advanced, extreme, and brilliant creation of the Devil," because, in his view, it purports to bring progress to society but actually does the opposite, resulting in a lack of creativity (18). It involves an "overreliance on comfort" and buries us under "lava flows of data" (138). The control and conformity-producing influence of any force—government, media, architecture, or technology—was, to Mailer, the chief threat to the freedom and creativity of the individual.

In an effort to combat the totalitarianism he witnessed in society, Mailer turned to theories of existentialism in his writing and in his personal philosophy. Though as a young man Mailer maintained atheistic beliefs, his ideas shifted in the mid-1950s, and his evolving theory of existentialism became intricately tied to his developing spiritual ideology, which by the 1960s was shaping most of his writing. While he borrowed ideas from famed existential theorists like Kierkegaard and Sartre, Mailer formulated his own unique brand of existentialism, one that included the possibility of a God. In *Advertisements for Myself,* Mailer expresses his belief that to be a "real" existentialist, one must "be religious" and have a sense of purpose that is grounded in the notion of a "meaningful but mysterious end" (341). This was the crux of existentialism in Mailer's mind: the ability to face down the unknown with courage, and to live with the knowledge that we cannot know what lies in front of us. As he would later clarify in *On God,* "To say 'existential' means you are in the midst of an activity to which you cannot see the result. Rather, you are living in the midst of an intense question" (44).[18]

This religious philosophy that informed his existentialism, a philosophy that traverses the terrains of both Manichaeism and Gnosticism but refuses to situate itself firmly in either camp, is a central focus of much of his work. The Manichaean inflection of his philosophy is evident in Mailer's belief in an ongoing battle between God and the devil, and this emphasis on dualism is reflected throughout his canon. Mailer believed in a "humanized" God with flaws that made divine power vulnerable to evil influence. In *The Presidential Papers,* a collection of essays and excerpts published in 1963, he summarizes his belief in this enduring conflict: "If God is not all powerful but existential, discovering the possibilities and limitations of his creative powers in the form of the history which is made by His creatures, then one must postulate an existential equal to God, an antagonist, the Devil, a principle of Evil whose signature was the concentration camps, whose joy is to waste substance, whose intent is to prevent God's conception of being from reaching its mysterious goal" (193). However, while traditional Manichaean philosophy posits that forces of good—those on the side of God—will ultimately win the battle, Mailer repeatedly argues that we cannot know the end. Thus, as he and Lennon also discuss in *On God,* his religious philosophy is perhaps closer to Gnosticism, which is also dualistic, but allows for the kind of existential unknowability that Mailer emphasized throughout his career. As he notes, "it isn't that we are passive onlookers while God and the Devil wage a war within us. We are the third force and don't always know which side we are on in any moment, or whether on another occasion we are independent of both."[19]

In yet another example of the way Mailer hybridizes ideas in his life and work, his spirituality is infused not only with Manichaeism and Gnosticism but also with Judaism. Raised in a Jewish family, Mailer himself never accepted the traditional Judaism practiced by his parents, and (with the possible exception of *The Naked and the Dead*), his work does not address the lives of Jewish Americans as explicitly as some contemporary Jewish writers, such as Philip Roth, Bernard Malamud, and Saul Bellow. Yet, as Michael Glenday notes, even though his work "shows few explicit signs of a self-conscious Jewish sensibility at work . . . it is possible to see Mailer is most Jewish even in this apparent rejection of traditional ties."[20] Mailer himself insisted that the religious and spiritual aspects of Judaism as well as the experience of Jewish identity were central to his work. Shortly before his death in 2007, in an interview for *Nextbook Reader,* Mailer was asked what role Judaism had played in his body of work. His response was, "An enormous role."[21] In a 1979 letter to Jack Abbott, with whom Mailer struck up his ultimately ill-fated friendship, Mailer wrote passionately about the presence of Jewish history in his own life. "Just as I don't know what it is to be a convict, you the fuck don't know what it is to be a Jew," he wrote after reading Abbott's comments on Israel. "You don't know what it is to have six million of your people killed when there are only twelve million of them on earth. You don't know the profound and fundamental stunting of existence that got into the blood cells of every Jew after Hitler had done his work."[22] Earlier in his life, Mailer had also explained that, "if my knowledge of Jewish culture is exceptionally spotty, as indeed it is, I am not so sure that that isn't an advantage in creating a modern American Jew. Because *his* knowledge of Jewish culture is also extremely spotty, and the way in which his personality is composed may be more in accordance with my ignorance."[23] As Mashey Bernstein has noted, "Mailer's ideology, as an American writer and social commentator, stems from the activist or prophetic side of Judaism. Despite the sometimes outrageous subject matter and highly charged sexual content, Mailer's novels and essays reflect a highly moral approach to life."[24]

In fact, one of the abiding concerns Mailer espouses throughout his body of work is the moral center—or lack thereof—of America at large. This does not mean that Mailer was a didactic moralist; rather, Mailer's definitions of morality, as expressed in both his fiction and his nonfiction, are unique and sometimes controversial, and do not lend themselves to the neat packaging often presented by organized religions or theologies. As Mailer stated, "The best fiction has always been the seedbed for the most interesting and subtle moral questions, questions that, at best, go deeper than the wisdom you can receive in any church or synagogue or mosque. . . . Interesting morality almost never fits prearranged moral codes."[25] Still, what Mashey Bernstein has referred to as a "highly moral approach to life" can be seen in nearly every one of his works, particularly in those where Mailer grapples with the nature of good and evil, seeking to make sense of the tragedy and corruption he sees around him. Of course, the "outrageous subject matter and highly charged sexual content" to which Bernstein also refers sometimes prevented readers from locating Mailer's very real concern with morality and spirituality. Nevertheless, Mailer feared for the moral and spiritual fate of America, and his literature often reflects individuals teetering on the precipice of crisis as they attempt to wade through a morally decaying society, which Mailer often described as "cancerous."

Violence, Masculinity, and Existential Courage

In Mailer's view, totalitarianism contributes to this social cancer, as do conformity, apathy, and cowardice. Individual courage, a key aspect of his existential philosophy, is often framed as an avenue through such "cancers." Thus the courageous, if tortured, existential masculine protagonist becomes a key figure in much of Mailer's fiction and nonfiction. In *The Presidential Papers,* Mailer indicated his belief that courage and risk-taking form the foundation of an existential masculine leadership, and that this "manly" existential leader would "create a new reality which would displace the old psychological reality" (26). He urges America to encourage "complexities" (which he also problematically calls "a manly activity") in their leaders, for it is only by doing so that the country will find the leader they need to flourish. This idea of complexity and risk-taking, as well as the necessity of replacing an old and decaying "psychological reality" with one that welcomes the possibility of regenerative violence, form the basis for Stephen Rojack's perceptions of desirable masculinity in *An American Dream,* a novel serialized over eight months in *Esquire* in 1964 before its publication as a novel in a slightly revised form in 1965—arguably one of Mailer's best but also most difficult novels in its treatment of ethics and morality.

Mailer meditates often—in his fiction, nonfiction, and interviews—about the role of violence in these constructions of an existential manhood. His ideas about violence change over the course of his career, and thus his musings on the subject more closely resemble an ongoing dialogue with his readers—and himself. In *A Calculus at Heaven,* for instance, one of Mailer's military heroes expresses his belief that "life and death and violent action were fundamentals, and he would find no lie there," a line that forms the basic foundation of much of Mailer's masculine ideology.[26] Later, in "The White Negro," he frames violence more specifically as an essential part of "Hip" masculinity. In a 1964 interview, Mailer also argues that individual violence is an essential response to the "extinction of possibilities," and claims that those who understand this can experience not only liberation, but also revelation.[27] For Mailer, individual violence, under the right circumstances, had the potential to be freeing, to assist the individual in working against cultural oppression and repression that often stemmed from totalitarian forces.

Of course, Mailer emphasizes early on that not all violence can be condoned. In the 1960s he begins to more clearly articulate a distinction between various forms of violence, clarifying that he disapproves of "*inhuman* violence—violence which is on a large scale and abstract."[28] Moreover, in works like *An American Dream* and 1967's *Why Are We in Vietnam?* he examines the negative consequences of individual violence, particularly when it is used as a misguided way to assert masculinity. By the end of his career, in *On God,* Mailer's views of individual violence are more tempered and even more articulate. There, for example, in response to Michael Lennon's remark that the Gospel of Thomas states that we must "bring forth what is within" or repression will destroy us, Mailer replies, "I used to believe that entirely. I now think it to be generally true but risky. Because what does it mean to bring forth what is within? I work on the notion that there's godliness within us and diabolism as well. So to bring forth what is within you, it is necessary, very often, to send out the worst elements of yourself," and often "what comes out is so bad that it injures others, sometimes dreadfully" (67). In spite of—or perhaps because of—these gradual evolutions and complexities in his views of violence, and the ethical gray areas these views inhabit, the theme of violence in Mailer's works has been a significant contributing factor to the controversy surrounding his writing. In an interview with Barry Leeds, Mailer himself said, "I think [my books] are doubly disturbing because what I am saying is: Look, I'm not asking you to read about violence so you can have a good read, I'm saying there's a whole lot of meaning in violence. That it's one aspect of a world-wide violence which appropriates us."[29]

While Mailer has become a somewhat notorious figure for his views and for his unapologetic manner of offering them, what comes across most evidently in his fiction, his nonfiction, his letters, and his public battles is that he loved an argument. Mailer enjoyed playing devil's advocate both in his debates (such as the famous "Town Bloody Hall" panel on feminism in 1971) as well as in his writing, wherein he remained devoted to considering all sides and perspectives of a variety of complex issues, from American politics to media to literature to identity. In *City of Words* Tony Tanner speaks to this dialectic in terms of Mailer's narrative style, arguing that in his fiction Mailer is perpetually negotiating between two worlds, and that his narrative voice often "calls into question its own theories" and "mocks its own metaphors and notions of magic."[30] This commitment to questioning, to skepticism, and to intellectual curiosity is apparent throughout Mailer's work, and Mailer believed this was part of his vocation as a writer. He believed that a writer was endowed with certain special, mystical qualities, and thus it was that writer's specific ethical responsibility to pursue truth and defy the negative consequences of complacency and conformity. He expresses as much in a 2007 interview with Andrew O'Hagan in the *The Paris Review,* in which he speaks of writing as a vocation that can often deplete rather than augment the ego. When O'Hagan asks Mailer whether he believes writing "is a sort of self-annihilation," Mailer promptly responds in the affirmative, claiming, "there's simply less of you after you finish a book."[31]

Such self-annihilation demands self-invention as well, something Mailer practiced throughout his career as he continually revised, rearticulated, and reshaped his ideas. As Mark Edmundson notes, "Of all the major American writers at work now, Norman Mailer probably has come the closest to committing himself to Emerson's literary ethos of self-destroying self-invention. From early on in his career it has been Mailer's aim to baffle expectations about who he is and what he might be capable of doing. His ambition has been thoroughly

Emersonian—'to dive and reappear in new places.'"[32] For this reason, Mailer's work can be complex and difficult, its sheer size and range sometimes daunting to a new reader. As John Whalen-Bridge remarked, Mailer was a writer "so rich that he gave us a kind of cultural indigestion."[33] Yet working to understand Mailer in all of his complexity—from his flawed but introspective theories of gender, to his unique spiritualism, to the tough love he displayed toward his country, to his untiring quest to push his readers and audience to be smarter and deeper thinkers—is enriching in its depth and challenge.

CHAPTER 2

The Naked and the Dead and Its Aftermath

In 1948, Mailer published *The Naked and the Dead,* which became an immediate success and introduced Mailer as a formidable presence on the American literary scene, launching his career as one of America's foremost authors and cultural commentators.[1] The novel, based on Mailer's own experiences as a private stationed in the Philippines during World War II, follows the journey of the 112th Cavalry Regiment as they embark on a reconnaissance mission around a fictional South Pacific island called Anopopei. The mission itself, along with the ensemble cast of soldiers, is also fictionalized, though many of the characters are based on specific men Mailer himself knew during the war. Selling over 200,000 copies in its first three months, the novel remained on the *New York Times* best-seller list for over a year and received wide critical acclaim; indeed, it is considered by many to be one of Mailer's most laudable works. David Dempsey in the *New York Times* called it "the most ambitious novel to be written about the recent conflict" of World War II and "the most ruthlessly honest"; and Raymond Rosenthal of *Commentary* noted that the novel was a "relief" after the "pussyfooting" of his contemporaries, who "ducked the reality" of war.[2]

While critics praised the freshness and honesty of Mailer's novel, they also pointed out the evident influence of writers like John Dos Passos, James T. Farrell, and Ernest Hemingway—authors also known for their incisive commentary on America, and America at war, specifically. As Philip Bufithis has noted, Hemingway's influence is particularly apparent in the "admiration of physical courage," "dark fatalism," and "naturalism" present in the novel.[3] Despite the apparent influence, Mailer's style in *The Naked and the Dead* is no mere imitation. As Vincent Casaregola has observed, rather than Hemingway's "iceberg theory," what we have in *The Naked and the Dead* is "a vast ice sheet."[4] Indeed,

Mailer delves deeply into his characters' psyches, offering detailed explanations of their histories, their feelings, and their motivations.

Moreover, *The Naked and the Dead* focuses its attention on many of the refrains that Mailer would consistently address throughout his career, including the construction of masculine identity, the threat of totalitarianism, and the nature of violence. The novel's complex exploration of masculinity is one of its most salient themes, and on this subject it provides a complement—and in some other cases, a contrast—to the ways Mailer tackles the issue of gender in his ensuing works. That is, while in later years Mailer would often be criticized for being insufficiently critical of his protagonists' hypermasculinity, in his debut novel there is an undeniable undercurrent of criticism with regard to the "machismo" on display in the army, and a more direct attempt to present certain aspects of masculinity as a guise. Mailer makes no moves, for instance, to downplay the acute fear each soldier experiences, and the veil of machismo worn by so many of his later characters is much more transparent here.

Some of this might be due to another of the novel's literary influences. In a 1998 introduction to the anniversary edition of the book, Mailer confessed that Tolstoy had been a significant influence on his writing at the time, and that the novel thus reflects a "Tolstoyan compassion." Mailer defines this compassion as the ability to "perceive everything that is good and bad about a character" but still "feel that the sum of us as human beings is probably a little more good than awful" (xii).[5] This "Tolstoyan compassion" is particularly evident in the sympathetic way he crafts the inner lives of the individual soldiers in the novel. While the protagonists of Mailer's later fiction are also granted depth and complexity of character, the cast of male characters in *The Naked and the Dead* seems to be allowed more vulnerability, and this vulnerability is treated with more concentrated, obvious empathy.

This is made particularly evident by Mailer's illumination of many of his main characters' psyches: the "secret fear" and "bottomless dread" Red Valsen feels in the aftermath of another young soldier's sudden death, the detailed description of Roth's paranoia during his night watch, and the high-running tensions among the soldiers themselves as they vacillate between deeply felt camaraderie and hatred for one another (123). And as Mailer spends a significant amount of time meditating on the meaning of masculinity, he acknowledges the pressure these young soldiers feel to prove themselves as men—to each other, to their superiors, and to their country. Private Stanley recounts the anxieties of being married young, only just coming to realize the vulnerabilities that, paradoxically, have been exposed by his overly confident ego. As Mailer writes of Stanley, "His love spasms had been quick and nervous; he had wept once or twice in his wife's arms at his failure. He had married so young because he was in love, but also because he had felt cocky and confident" (294). This commentary is offered without judgment or criticism by any narrative voice. Rather, the honesty and youthful angst with which such statements are offered invites empathy. Such an authorial tone makes it surprising that Mailer wrote the novel when he was only twenty-four, as the self-awareness with which he imbues his characters suggests an author looking back on his youth after many years of hindsight.

The difficulty in defining and coming to terms with the notion of one's "masculine" duties, particularly for young men who have only just reached adulthood before being sent to war, is also evident in the narrative of enlisted soldier Roy Gallagher. One evening, Gallagher finds himself thinking of his pregnant wife at home, trying and failing to draw up a clear image of her face. All the while, he is also meditating on his responsibilities as a husband and father as he tries to keep up with his duties as a soldier, but "all he could feel was a sense of guilt. . . . No matter what he tried, no matter how hard he worked, he seemed always to be caught." As a result, his "bitterness became sharper, flooded him for a moment" (6). Gallagher's guilt arises not only from his inability to recall the specific details of his wife's features, but from his inability to determine whether his duties as a husband and a soldier are in a state of conflict, for in fulfilling one role he seems to fail in the other. His thoughts highlight a distinct anxiety over the notion that he is trapped in a role he has not yet figured out how to fulfill. He loves his wife, but feels "caught" by their marriage, and is ensnared in a cycle of guilt. When his wife dies in childbirth soon afterward, Gallagher comes undone, unraveling as he continues to receive letters from her, postmarked before her death but delayed by the wartime mail system. As a result, he finds himself in a time warp of sorts, haunted by his dead wife's missives. The men in his platoon watch him grieve with silent, nonjudgmental, and heartbreaking sympathy, exhibiting the kind of "Tolstoyan compassion" that drives the narrative.

The centrality of this kind of human vulnerability and compassion is complicated, however, by the characterizations of two central figures in the platoon: Sergeant Croft and General Cummings. Croft is a man who "loves combat" (17) and who believes that "a man who was afraid to put his neck out on the line was no damn good" (28). As a courageous leader, and one who has worked hard for the fear and respect of his men, Croft exemplifies a notion of masculine courage that Mailer continued to develop (albeit with slightly more nuance) throughout his later career. In one of the novel's ten "Time Machine" segments, in which Mailer provides details about the soldiers' lives before the war, Croft is described as "efficient and strong and usually empty and his main cast of mind was a superior contempt toward nearly all other men. He hated weakness and he loved practically nothing. There was a crude unformed vision in his soul but he was rarely conscious of it" (156).

In a move that demonstrates a touch of compassion, however, whereby he seeks to understand all sides of the man, Mailer takes the time to explore *why* Croft harbors such a deep contempt, and why his soul contains little but a "crude unformed vision." He suggests, for instance, in a section titled "The Education of Samuel Croft," that Croft's behavior is a result of the environment in which he came of age, where topics of discussion were largely racist and misogynistic, and wherein Croft is encouraged to don a masculine identity protected by an impenetrable exterior of superiority and aggression. It is this attitude that leads him to describe everyone around him as "a bunch of fuggin whores," "a bunch of dogs," and "deer to track" (164).

Unlike many of the other soldiers, however, Croft's background story does not necessarily invite the reader to feel empathy for him; we are not quite "able to feel that the sum of us as human beings is probably a little more good than awful," the marker of a "Tolstoyan compassion," when observing the man he has become. Consider the moment, for instance, where Croft demonstrates what might be his most pointless act of cruelty, when he finds his men caring for a lost and injured baby bird. Roth, in particular, has "fallen in love" with the animal, as "all the frustrated affection he had stored for months seemed to pour out toward the bird" (529). The men's care for the bird is touching and understandable: this is perhaps the only life they feel they have the power or permission to save at this moment, and it is as though the human carnage surrounding them might be temporarily forgotten or redeemed so long as this one innocent creature survives. Yet Croft denies them this redemption, for when he takes the bird in his hand, the men suddenly hear "a little numbly the choked squeal of the bird, the sudden collapsing of its bones" (530). Though furious, the men are too afraid and dutiful to do anything that might be deemed mutinous. In one brief scene, then, Mailer is able to subtly allude to the pratfalls of a violent performance of masculinity, to the cruelty and corruption of leadership in the military, to the impotence of the individual enlisted soldier, and to the repression and redirection of a soldier's grief, tragedy, and guilt.

General Edward Cummings is a similarly difficult character, talented and respected as a strategist but disliked for his elitism and reinforcement of officer privilege. He too is given further depth by the history provided in his own "Time Machine" segment, which is tellingly subtitled, "A Peculiarly American Statement." Here, it is revealed that Cummings's mother encouraged him in artistic endeavors as a child until his tyrannical father, put off by his son's involvement in traditionally feminized activities, intervenes and forces Cummings to join the military, where he will supposedly learn to "start thinking how to act like a man" (407) and stop "actin' like a goddam woman" (405). By providing information regarding Cummings's childhood, Mailer paints the general in his youth as a sympathetic character, a victim of his father's own flawed notion of gender. We see the hypermasculine father figure as the villain, not the model, whose insecurity with regard to his own gendered identity is revealed in his irrational fear that his son will be less of a man should he pursue art as opposed to violence.

While the military does change Cummings, as his father had hoped, Mailer makes it clear that he too is no exemplar of ideal masculinity: he is alternately cold, obsessively compulsive, and deeply unhappy. On the surface, he may appeal to his father's notions of manhood, but the "peculiarly American" dilemma he faces encompasses the unnatural struggle to be that stoic, aggressive, individualistic man so lauded by both his family and country. His clear discomfort within this role is proof that such a performance of masculinity, particularly when disingenuous and forced, is deeply flawed as a paradigm. Cummings's transformation is perhaps more tragic because we as readers can see he has the intellect and ability to question the masculine role he has been assigned, yet fails to do so.

The complex interactions among the characters themselves further contribute to the commentary on the concept of masculinity, maturity, and war. Mailer spends much of the novel exploring the fraught relationships between the men in the platoon, often highlighting the tensions that arise among them as a result of fatigue, fear, insecurity, anger, and guilt—tensions that occasionally play out in aggressive confrontations. One of the most unique relationships between soldiers in the novel is that of General Cummings and Lieutenant Hearn. Hearn, the General's aide and "right-hand man," respects Cummings for his efficiency and expertise, but also resents him for his condescension, stubbornness, and snobbery. The two men struggle with a paradoxical combination of respect and loathing for one another, and are engaged in a silent but ongoing battle of egos, though this traditional masculine competitiveness is tinged with an increasingly evident sexual tension between the two men. Hearn seems more than vaguely aware of the General's desire for him; at one point, he observes that Cummings "owned, no doubt, most of the dirty little itches, the lusts for things which were unacceptable to the mores of the weekly slick-paper magazines" (79). These "dirty little itches," we can infer, include his sexual attraction to Hearn, at the time considered a social taboo, particularly in a military environment that impressed upon men the value and necessity of heteronormativity.[6]

Other moments find the two men engaged in physical encounters during which the sexual tension is palpable. Consider, for instance, the following scene: "At the entrance to the General's tent, another collision occurred. Hearn halted at the tent flaps to allow the General to precede him, and Cummings in turn put his hand on Hearn's back to indicate that he was to go first. They both started at once, and Hearn sideswiped the General, felt him recoil a foot or two from the weight of Hearn's big body" (171). This tenuous attraction culminates in a chess game that is fraught not only with masculine competitiveness, but distinct desire; at the end of the game, Hearn confesses that "he had an intuition that if he remained motionless long enough the General would slowly extend his arm, touch his knee perhaps" (182). Yet for both men, the desire is tinged with resentment. Hearn realizes, for example, that for Cummings, "he had been the pet, the dog, to the master, coddled and curried, thrown sweetmeats until he had had the presumption to bite the master once" (313). Eventually, the tension between the two men increases to such a degree that Cummings reassigns Hearn to a different unit, in an attempt to eradicate his complicated loathing of Hearn and of himself.

That Hearn dies as an indirect result of this reassignment—shot by the Japanese after Croft suppresses intel that might have saved him—is tragically significant, for despite his troubled relationship with Cummings, Hearn had been the most promising leader among the officers, intelligent and adept at his job, but lacking the ingrained coldness and cruelty of Cummings and Croft. As Nigel Leigh argues, "the political implications of [Hearn's] death are profoundly pessimistic" for "the most enlightened position in the novel has been shown to be insubstantial"; Randall Waldron adds that his death "dramatize[s] the defeat of man by the machine."[7] Yet this potential pessimism should not be mistaken for nihilism or futility. In an interview with Lillian Ross directly after the novel's publication, Mailer says, "People say it is a novel without hope. . . . Actually, it offers a great deal of hope. . . . The book finds man corrupted, confused to the point of helplessness, but it also finds that there are limits beyond which he cannot be pushed, and it finds that even in his corruption and sickness there are yearnings for a better world."[8]

This clash of hopeful optimism and stark realities is also evident within Mailer's depiction of Roth and Goldstein, the two Jewish characters in the novel, who also serve as vehicles for a consideration of the impact of race and ethnicity on masculine identity. While references to Judaism and Jewish identity appear in Mailer's later work, nowhere is his meditation on Jewish identity so overt as in this first novel. In fact, as Ezra Cappell has argued, this is one of the ways that Mailer steps out and away from Hemingway's long shadow, for "far from slavishly following Ernest Hemingway's anti-Semitic lead," Mailer offers a "complex portrait of Jewish characters attempting to negotiate the constraints of an anti-Semitic, mid-century America."[9] At least part of this emphasis is a result of the novel's context: set amid the conflict of World War II and written and published amid the discoveries of the atrocities of the Holocaust, it is unsurprising that Mailer would concern himself with the pervasive anti-Semitism within the American military. There are many references to the overtly anti-Semitic comments to which Roth and Goldstein are regularly subjected. For instance, after finding out his wife died in childbirth, Gallagher says, "I bet a fuggin Yid was the doctor" (265). Goldstein overhears soldiers saying, "Just hope you all don't get in F Company, that's where they stick the goddam Jewboys" (53), and he later recognizes that, in the army, "A Jew was a punching bag because they could not do without one" (662).

However, Mailer's depiction of the experiences of Jewish characters also raises larger questions about how race and ethnicity are woven into—or left out of—culturally enforced notions of masculinity and American identity. For example, Roth and Goldstein represent the ways that men who did not fit the white heteronormative standard were emasculated, their gendered identities negatively branded by the racialization and feminization of their Jewish identities.[10] When Goldstein complains about the poor management of the platoon's mission, for instance, the following exchange ensues:

> "You bitching again, Goldstein?" Croft asked.
>
> The anti-Semite, Goldstein thought. "I'm just expressing my opinion," he said.
>
> "Opinion!" Croft spat. "A bunch of goddam women have opinions." (127)

The fear of being stereotyped based on his religious and cultural background is also what makes Roth keep his distance from Goldstein, despite his concession that "a Jew always had to go to a fellow Jew to find understanding" (56).

Mailer does not relegate his exploration of race in America to his depiction of anti-Semitism, however. Martinez, the Mexican-born scout for the platoon, also faces disrespect from other enlisted men who refuse to take orders from a Mexican soldier. Moreover, his "Time Machine" segment also refers to the wider discrimination he will continue to face in America. There, Mailer writes: "Little Mexican boys also breathe the American fables. If they cannot be aviators or financiers or officers they can still be heroes. No need to stumble over pebbles and search the Texas sky. Any man jack can be a hero. Only that does not make you white Protestant, firm and aloof" (67). Here, through Martinez, Mailer both affirms and criticizes notions of the American Dream: in America, Martinez may have opportunities that he would not have in Mexico, but that will not make him equal in the eyes of an America whose power structure is still founded in white Christian hegemony. He might be a hero, but he may never be deemed an *American* hero.

In fact, Mailer also uses several of his characters in *The Naked and the Dead* to question notions of heroism in general, which in turn allows him to reveal the demoralizing banality of war. For example, a young soldier named Buddy Wyman admits that, when he joined the army, he "had vague dreams about being a hero, assuming this would bring him some immense reward which would ease his life" (134). He also explains that he had "always imagined combat as exciting, with no misery and no physical exertion. He dreamed of himself charging across a field in the face of many machine guns; but in the dream there was no stitch in his side from running too far while bearing too much weight" (134). By contrasting Wyman's fantasy with the reality of the situation—the excruciating physical trials and drudgery of the reconnaissance mission—Mailer undermines the notion that there might be some sort of idealistic heroism conferred by wartime combat. As a result, Mailer's depiction of war seems gloomier but more honest, as his novel depicts the reality of war for those men who see combat only infrequently, and for whom real pain comes from a constant, tortuous discomfort and persistent fear of death amid the ominous quietude of the jungle.

In his ongoing examination of the complexity of wartime heroism, Mailer also uses his characters to acknowledge that wartime experience can be instructive even as it undoes notions of individual glory. For example, for Cummings, war is a sexualized, spiritual experience that teaches man about the darkest parts of himself, even amid the day-to-day triviality. As he thinks, war "was all covered with tedium and routine, regulations and procedure, and yet there was a naked quivering heart to it which involved you deeply when you were thrust into it. All the deep dark urges of man, the sacrifices on the hilltop, and the churning lusts of the night and sleep, weren't all of them contained in the shattering screaming burst of a shell, the man-made thunder and light?" (566). Though Cummings is a character with whom it is difficult to identify, it is possible to appreciate his illumination of the darker aspects of war here, as he recognizes the ways in which the universe of war is stripped of the veneer of "civilized society" and thus brings out what might be termed our baser, more primitive, more emotive instincts.

Cummings's meditations also point to the larger, more devastating consequences of war on the individual human psyche. For Cummings, war is a living, breathing entity in itself; he later compares weapons to humans, writing about them in a poetic and highly erotic manner, describing "the phallus shell that rides through a shining vagina of steel, soars through the sky, and then ignites into earth" (568). In contrast to the weapons, which are personified here and seem to take on a life of their own, in war "men are closer to machines than humans" (569). By imbuing Cummings with these thoughts, Mailer is able to comment on the ease with which men can be overtaken by the violence of war, which becomes a being in and of itself, its power and allure eventually snowballing until the individual becomes obsolete. This overpowering influence of war is also driven home at the end of the novel, wherein the futility of individual action is emphasized as the men discover that their patrol, which resulted in the deaths of Hearn, Roth, and fellow soldier Woodrow Wilson, was largely useless—the soldiers at the front line having successfully defeated the enemy while the reconnaissance platoon was on their mission, thus rendering it unnecessary before it had barely begun. The relative insignificance of the individual is emphasized when Nature's power over man is revealed: while attempting to march up a mountain on Anopopei, the members of the platoon find themselves unexpectedly driven off a mountain by a swarm of hornets (an event Mailer drew from a real wartime experience). These kinds of anticlimactic devices are likely what led David Dempsey to conclude that Mailer's narrative was "the most ruthlessly honest" account of war. Though Mailer manages to convey sympathy and respect for each of the characters he fashions here, this is no glorified portrait of war, but one that examines its complexities and moral gray areas.

Embedded in this critique is also a comment on the bureaucratic and political corruption that feeds wartime conflict.[11] This is thrown into stark relief during the conversations between General Cummings and Lieutenant Hearn. "You can't begin to imagine how effective the Big Lie is," Cummings says to Hearn. "Your average man never dares suspect that the men in power have all the nasty impulses he has, except they're more effective about carrying them out. . . . We're all guilty, that's the truth" (313). Here, the "Big Lie" could be any number of things: that all actions of war are justified, that war makes all men heroes, that those in power are certain and confident in all of their decisions, that leaders are righteous and uncorrupted, that the officers know more than their men, or all of the above. Through Cummings, Mailer is also able to hypothesize about the origins of corruption in particular, suggesting that many military decisions are driven by the individual ego—the need to feel one's power in a world that is constantly calling individual power into question. "When we come kicking into the world, we *are* God, the universe is the limit of our senses," says Cummings. "And when we get older, when we discover that the universe is not us, it's the deepest trauma of our existence" (323).

Cummings further observes that the fascism against which American forces are fighting is actually "grounded firmly in men's actual natures" and "merely started in the wrong country"; in his mind, America is going to "absorb" the dream of fascism that Germany attempted to execute, because "when you've created power, materials, armies, they don't wither of their own accord" (321). In part, what Cummings's hypothesis suggests is that, while America might not identify as a fascist nation, it too is largely concerned with power—America fights in the name of democracy and may be in the process of abolishing a real evil, but the lust for power will remain.

In voicing this idea through Cummings, Mailer is able to allude to the totalitarian forces that might potentially arise from a war that aims to demolish those very forces.[12] The novel does not assume, however, that such a development is inevitable or insurmountable. Rather, Mailer uses his characters to depict the merits—indeed the necessity—of maintaining an investment in the ideology of existential freedom. As Raymond Wilson notes, "Mailer does not depict people incapable of freedom in the face of powerful influences; rather he creates characters who have given up their freedom in a complex process that arises from their embracing the unrealistic American myth of success" and who "reinterpret the myth in a direction that favors subservience to a structure."[13] Indeed, as Mailer would state much later in life, "Myths are tonic to a nation's heart. Once abused, however, they are poisonous."[14] Some might argue that the novel's context demands such patriotism and subservience; after all, rebellion against the military structure during wartime would cause chaos and, perhaps, failure in the military's larger mission. Yet the kind of power Mailer addresses—and that to which Wilson alludes in his reading of the novel—has more to do with the pervasive authoritarian structures in America than the day-to-day hierarchy of the military. That is, Mailer seems more concerned with the ways wartime ideology and the quest for power might corrupt men both during and after the war, leading to an increasingly totalitarian power structure. His main concern, in other words, is what the power arising from the "absorption" of fascism might do to America, particularly the American individual.

This obsession with power and the looming threat of fascism's energy is also connected to the complex nature of violence. Throughout his career, Mailer continued to examine the presence and repercussions of both individual and mass violence in both his fiction and his nonfiction. The seeds of his distinction between these types of violence, though, can be found in *The Naked and the Dead,* for here Mailer makes it clear that individual violence—though it may always have negative consequences—can be explained and even justified by personal history and circumstance, while mass violence, particularly that borne of totalitarianism, cannot. Mailer clarifies this distinction—and his own attitude about violence while writing his first novel—in an interview with Paul Krassner for *The Realist* in 1962. There, he notes: "Beneath the ideology in *The*

Naked and the Dead was an obsession with violence. The characters for whom I had the most secret admiration, like Croft, were violent people. Ideologically, intellectually, I did disapprove of violence. . . . what I still disapprove of is *inhuman* violence—violence which is on a large scale and abstract. I disapprove of bombing a city. I disapprove of the kind of man who will derive aesthetic satisfaction from the fact that an Ethiopian village looks like a red rose at the moment the bombs are exploding."[15]

Thus, while Mailer clearly believed in the power of violence, he also saw the damage that might result when it is adopted as a mechanism of social control, as evidenced by his distinction between "human" and "inhuman" violence. He was against institutional and ideological violences (like totalitarianism and fascism) that oppress the individual, as well as massive acts of horrific violence that derive from these ideologies (like that of the Holocaust). It is this large-scale ideological violence, in particular, that he interrogates in *The Naked and the Dead*. He not only examines its gory global consequences, but also the consequences of oppressive institutionalized violences like racism, anti-Semitism, homophobia, sexism, classism, and totalitarianism on the psyche and development of the individual soldier. Thus, to deem *The Naked and the Dead* as a "war novel" would be to vastly oversimplify its content, for while it is a compelling account of one platoon's wartime experience, it delves much further into the problems of individual oppression, existential dilemmas, and the impact of gendered and racial identities in America.

Barbary Shore, Mailer's next literary effort following *The Naked and the Dead,* was not nearly as critically lauded as his debut novel, nor did it sell as many copies. In fact, upon its publication in 1951, *Barbary Shore* elicited some of the worst reviews of Mailer's career, and the negative reception served a significant blow to his ego. The less enthusiastic response can be attributed to a number of factors. Stylistically, it differs greatly from *The Naked and the Dead,* so readers looking for more of the same would have been somewhat disappointed. Moreover, as part of a political allegory, the novel's highly symbolic language has an alienating effect, making it more difficult to identify with characters who come across as abstractions rather than fully developed personalities. The novel centers on the experiences of a shell-shocked aspiring novelist, Mike Lovett, who becomes enmeshed in a political conspiracy while living in a boardinghouse. While there, he comes in contact with a number of his odd neighbors, including the reclusive author McLeod, the provocative and somewhat tempestuous landlady Guinevere, her precocious daughter Monina, and the youthful but jaded undercover FBI agent Hollingsworth. Lovett (correctly) predicts all of these acquaintances to be involved in a conspiracy in which he has become unwillingly and unwittingly involved. However, the actual nature of their political intrigue remains elusive, and the novel develops into a meditation on socialist political philosophy, articulated within long conversations among Hollingsworth, Lovett, and McLeod. Moreover, due to the nature of the characters, whose motives are either questionable or absent, as well as various confusions in the plot, the novel often reads more like the explication of a theory via narrative than a novel.[16]

To be fair, however, that was Mailer's goal. In other words, his aim in *Barbary Shore* was not to create a campy "whodunit" or a "page-turner" (great novels, Mailer once said, are "not good page turners"); rather, it was to present a serious conversation about the instability and corruption within America.[17] Moreover, the book allows Mailer to work through some of the ideologies and political philosophies that shaped his later work. Mailer spends a significant amount of time in *Barbary Shore* exploring Marxist theory, experimenting with the notion that this particular political philosophy might provide answers to the problems of totalitarianism, conformity, corruption, consumerism, and repression he observed in society. Most often, he uses McLeod as a mouthpiece for this idea, for McLeod not only displays an investment in Marxist ideals, but (in a reflection of the relationship between Mailer and his then-mentor Jean Malaquais) teaches them to the novel's younger, more naive protagonist. "There is the worker and the machine," McLeod informs Lovett, "and as the machine grows larger the man diminishes until one can hear from the background the funereal hymn of the falling rate with the sense it gives that what is born must die and yet grows larger before it expires" (216). This fear that an authoritative, totalitarian "machine" would encourage conformity and wipe out individual creativity is evoked in many of Mailer's later works, as Mailer felt throughout his life that this was the defining threat of contemporary American society. As he would later reflect, in *Barbary Shore* he may have been "trying for something which was at the very end of my reach, and then beyond it, and toward the end the novel collapsed into a chapter of political speech and never quite recovered." Nevertheless, he says, "it could be that if my work is alive one hundred years from now, *Barbary Shore* will be considered the richest of my first three novels for it has in its high fevers a kind of insane insight. . . . it has an air which for me is the air of our time, authority and nihilism stalking one another in the orgiastic hollow of this century."[18]

Fittingly, reflecting his perception of the hollowness and pessimism of the time, the characters in *Barbary Shore* do not trust one another, and we do not trust them, and this produces a distinctly unsettling effect—perhaps particularly so for readers at the time of the book's publication, who were living through the paranoia of the Red Scare, McCarthyism, and the onset of the

Korean War. As Norman Podhoretz notes, "Mailer's point in *Barbary Shore* is precisely that our society is *not* what it seems to be. . . . Mailer means to convey a sense of the strangeness of the way things are and to evoke a feeling for the overpowering reality of the invisible forces that supply a key to this strangeness."[19] This strangeness is conveyed most acutely by Lovett, who is suffering from a disorienting amnesia that leaves him without a past or a sense of real identity—a condition that is meant to symbolize the psychological state of modern man. As Lovett states, "The man lives in this city, but he has never seen these streets. The architecture is strange, and the people are dressed in unfamiliar clothing. He looks at a sign, but it is printed in an alphabet he cannot read" (6). Lovett serves as a kind of "everyman" for the modern era, lost and adrift; his amnesia acts as a somewhat heavy-handed metaphor for the larger problems that result from feeling disconnected from history and society—alienated from his fellow men, trapped in a world where "the details of my own history were lost in the other, common to us all" (4).

Through Lovett, Mailer ventriloquizes a fear of anonymity, of inaction, his journey representing modern man's attempt to reclaim some sense of individuality. Lannie, a fellow boarder, sees this alienation as a kind of narcissism: "the closer you come to the water the more you adore yourself until your nose touches, and then you're alone again," she says (154). By alluding to a modern-day Narcissus, Mailer can offer comment on the tendency of mankind to turn inward, toward self and solipsism, a situation that fuels his attempt to devise some kind of ideology that would unite people and encourage more rebellion against conformity.

The setting of the novel, elicited largely by the characters' bleak perspective of the world around them, contributes to this idea of social erosion, a decay that implicates everyone. Lovett, for instance, recalls: "So I stood at my distance above the river, and watched a dirty moon yellow the water. Somewhere, today, I had read in the newspaper, a woman had killed her children, and a movie star had enplaned from the West to be wed in a tiny church upon some hill. A boy had been found starving on a roof, a loaded rifle in his hands. The trigger squeezed, the shot rang down the street, and I could have been holding the rifle. I could even hate the boy because he had missed" (118). Lovett sees no beauty around him: the fabric of society has been torn by senseless violence and suffering, poorly stitched back together by even more senseless and inane celebrity news that is meant to disguise the more deeply affecting news of the day. Even the dirty moon and the yellow water suggest disease and decay.

Lannie, a frustrated Marxian idealist, perhaps most prominently embodies this cynical outlook, as her views also offer a hypothesis of where the world might end up if the individual simply gives in to apathy and the "machine."

According to Lannie, the modern world seems to be not only permanently marred but defined by the Holocaust, where people "went choking into the gas with the blood of a friend in their mouth," an occurrence which elicited a world where "there are no solutions, there are only exceptions, and therefore we are without good and evil" (213).[20] Lannie, a tragic, lonely figure, exemplifies the mentality of one who has ceased to take action and truly confront existential obstacles. Though acutely aware of what Mailer would call the world's cancerous state, and thus more enlightened than many around her, Lannie is not a model of the modern American individual, though she is a product of modern America. Indeed, many of the characters in the novel—even Lovett—feel responsibility and guilt for the failure to instigate a revolution against institutional fascism and cultural totalitarianism.

The desultory mood of the novel has elicited polarized responses over the years. An early reviewer for *Time,* for example, suggested that, in *Barbary Shore,* Mailer displays "a bad case of moral claustrophobia," and others similarly found fault with the overarching cynicism about moral and social decay in America. In a later analysis, however, David Anshen finds "a fervent wish for rebellion and struggle" which "gives early anticipation of the stance that Mailer will take in his later writings which often celebrate courage, or will and determination, as the road to existential authenticity and/or the basis for political rebellion."[21] In other words, Mailer's book might demonstrate a crescendo of amoral, erratic, or conformist behavior from his protagonists, which can be seen as a reaction to a continually failing cultural revolution, but his aim is not to point out such amorality and ambivalence and throw his hands up in despair; rather, as Anshen suggests, his aim might be to use this bleak setting as a call for ideological and political change.

Ultimately Mailer turned away from the idea that a single traditional ideology like Marxism can provide the "answer" to the world's problems—for him, such ideologies, political camps, and organized religions proved too restrictive and dogmatic. If there is any lasting ideology that comes out of this book, one that might be said to exist in Mailer's later work as well, it pertains more to his notion of the psychology of the individual. While referring to the relationship between the individual and a world that seems to exist separately, for instance, McLeod says, "One's psychological warp, upon which you harp so greedily, may be precisely the peculiar lens necessary to see those relations most clearly" (270). This idea—that a certain psychological "warp" is required in order to cut through the false surface of social relationships and see the reality of the world—is something Mailer explored pointedly in many of his later writings, particularly in his 1957 essay "The White Negro." Many of Mailer's protagonists, as well as the "real" people he profiles in his nonfiction, have what might be said to be a certain "warp," a strange insight that makes them magnetic despite their flaws, for they are shown to be able to see things that others—blinded by the corporate, conformist culture around them—cannot.

In *The Deer Park* (1955) Mailer continues to demonstrate his concern with what Norman Podhoretz deemed the "pathology of the modern spirit" that pervaded *Barbary Shore*.[22] *The Deer Park* chronicles several months in the life of former Air Force pilot Sergius O'Shaugnessy after his move to Desert D'Or, a remote town situated two hundred miles outside of Hollywood. The town is populated by an exclusive in-crowd of screenwriters, directors, actors, and actresses—some successful, some considered failures—along with their wealthy friends and patrons. Sergius, wracked with guilt as a result of his involvement in bombing missions that killed innocent civilians, is suffering from PTSD (a consequence of which has been an extended period of impotence). Due in part to his inner turmoil and aimlessness after active military duty, Sergius has chosen Desert D'Or as the place where he will spend a recent fortune of fourteen thousand dollars in gambling winnings until he decides what to do next. The town lends itself to this goal, defined as it is by a certain kind of excess—unsurprising, perhaps, because of the careers of its inhabitants—though interestingly, such wealth is not garishly displayed or even immediately visible. Sergius describes Desert D'Or as "a town built out of no other obvious motive than commercial profit and so no sign of commerce was allowed to appear," a state which will allow Sergius to live his temporarily directionless but comfortable life without drawing too much attention (7).[23]

The motley crew that populates Desert D'Or includes Dorothea O'Faye, the town matron; Dorothea's son Marion, an idle, arrogant, and cunning figure who makes his money working as the town pimp; Charles Eitel, a famous film director who is under investigation by the U.S. House Un-American Activities Committee for being a communist sympathizer ("Eitel" often being read as a play on "I tell"); Lulu Myers, the actress with whom Sergius falls in love; and Elena, Charles Eitel's lover, often considered one of Mailer's most fully developed (if somewhat tragic) female characters. The cast spends their time at an endless string of parties, the most notable of these held at the home of Dorothea O'Faye, and the quotidian is defined by its languid aimlessness—a mood that no doubt led Philip Bufithis to call the novel's atmosphere "purgatorial."[24]

This atmosphere appears perfectly suited to Sergius's temperament, yet he does not immediately feel at home in such an environment. He knows his looks, charm, and military credentials will allow him entry into the tightly knit society, but he is also fully aware that this appearance is a mere facade. "When

I would put on my uniform, I would feel like an unemployed actor who tries to interest a casting director by dressing for the role," he states (10). Indeed, as an orphan with no family, no roots, and no real sense of identity (a background strikingly similar to that of the similarly lost Mikey Lovett in *Barbary Shore*), Sergius says that, to some extent, he "had been faking all [his] life" (23).[25] Still, the appeal of Desert D'Or is that it will allow him to avoid a "real world" defined by wars "where orphans burned orphans"; the town exemplifies an "imaginary world" where, instead, "almost everybody lived" (45). Thus we can see that Sergius is faced from the very beginning with an existential crisis of identity: unsure of who he is and faced with the unknown, he chooses to turn his back on reality—a decision that seems destined to fail.

Through its focus on Sergius's existential dilemma, as well as its depiction of Charles Eitel's political and career struggles at middle age, *The Deer Park* also demonstrates Mailer's continued and related interest in the shape of American masculinity. These men, along with Marion Faye in a more supporting role, represent different facets of particularly gendered struggles. Sergius is the restless youth searching for some purpose, more akin to a Hemingway character—the post–World War II version of the "lost generation." He, like many of Mailer's and Hemingway's characters, also has a history that includes a brief affair with amateur boxing, which becomes a metaphor for his entry into masculinity and his attempt to earn some degree of masculine courage. However, as he notes, "After a while I realized I had no punch. . . . I can hardly tell you how I hated to admit to myself that I had no real punch. No *real* punch" (195). His instinct, rather than to be a fighter, is to be a writer—and thus, he becomes the novel's observer, the outsider who appraises those around him but who comes dangerously close to being swallowed up by the secluded life of Desert D'Or.

We meet Eitel, an older man, at a different stage of his life, but he too faces his own existential crisis of masculinity, as he seeks to maintain his virility, his clout, and his power amid an emerging government scandal and a toxic relationship with Elena, both of which leave him facing an unknown but ominous future. Much of Eitel's masculine crisis arises from the moral dilemma he faces in deciding whether to testify in front of the Communist-hunting congressional committee, but this crisis manifests itself as angry vitriol directed at Elena. Often, such anger also exposes his deep-seated vulnerability. At one point, he thinks, "If Elena had lied to him the way he had lied to her, had been with another man, washed, and come to his bed, he could have strangled her. . . . Abruptly, he recognized how completely he must own her. 'I'm willing to grant her no life at all,' Eitel said to himself, and with a sickly perspiration could only think, 'How I'm deteriorating, oh how I'm deteriorating'" (183).

This confession reflects both Eitel's need to maintain some semblance of decidedly masculine power, which is being threatened by job- and government-related pressures, as well as his awareness of the desperation and flaw of his need, particularly the double standard inherent in his attitude. He is haunted by the conflicted notion that he "must own" Elena in order to feel in control, but knows that the insecurity behind such desire also reflects the rapidity with which he is "deteriorating," a reference to age, psychological and emotional stress, and a fear of failure in Hollywood. It is an internal conflict that he does not fully resolve, though his journey throughout the novel is to search for some form of peace amid the task of rediscovering his place in the world.

As he works through his own mid-life crisis, Eitel is concurrently working on a play, and his dramatic hero serves as a kind of wry self-assessment of his own preoccupations. As Eitel explains, "My hero goes down to the bottom of the world and he wanders through the slums and the soup kitchens and the dreary cheap saloons . . . until in the anger of his chain of defeats he turns on them, he destroys himself with some pathetic violence, his sainthood remembered only by the despairing round of his sins" (111). Such a character not only serves a kind of cathartic function for Eitel, but also anticipates many of Mailer's later protagonists, who also aggressively fight against a sense of a decaying society with a violence that paradoxically ends up limiting them more than it liberates them.

Mailer's engagement with the anxieties of masculinity also plays out in the contrast between two of the novel's peripheral characters: Herman Teppis and Teddy Pope. Teppis, an aggressive Hollywood agent who manages the careers of Teddy and Lulu Meyers (and who has orchestrated a publicity stunt that presents them as a couple) is the epitome of hypermasculine bombast. Teddy, a more passive figure, has succumbed to Teppis's demands on his career and public image for some time before confessing that he is gay, and has no desire to marry Lulu for publicity. Teppis's response to Teddy's confession is to tell him he is a "coward" with "a chip against society" (231). As he goes on to say, "You should love society with all it's done for you. I love society. I respect it. Teddy, you're a sick boy, but you and me can lick this thing together" (231). Teppis's notion that same-sex desire is an insult to society, to Hollywood, and to himself—as well as his idea that Teddy can be "cured" of such an "affliction"—exemplifies his own homophobia as well as a prevailing attitude in America at the time. During a historical moment when any lifestyle or comment considered controversial meant persecution for alleged Communist sympathies, Teddy's admission is not only unique but also dangerous. By capturing his distress and sense of entrapment, Mailer captures the mood of the period, offering a cultural commentary on the factors bearing down on masculinity, and the ways in which masculinity could be denied by the heteronormative standard of that era.

In fact, no one seems at ease in this world, least of all the women. At one party, for example, Sergius sees "half a dozen women" whom he describes as "dressed expensively, and their makeup to make up for such faults as thin mouths, small eyes, and mouse-colored hair, had curved their lips, slimmed their cheeks, and given golden or chestnut tints to their coiffures. Like warriors behind their painted shields, they sat stiffly, three and three, starting at one another, talking with apathy" (62). Herman Teppis's daughter is described as having "pale haggard eyes"; "the bones of her chest stood out," and her voice was "pinched" (68). Elena, though a "near beauty," is "obviously not at ease" and looked like "an animal, ready for flight" (73). These women, too, hide behind their respective facades, which mask (or in some cases have entirely erased) any joy, buoyancy, or sense of self. Their function in the novel is similarly superficial: the women in *The Deer Park* are minor characters with little interior life, serving to illuminate the experience of the men in the novel. Even Elena's character, who is given perhaps the most depth, is certainly not a positive take on womanhood. Consider her reaction after being in a serious car accident: her first words are an apology to Eitel, and her next thoughts turn to wondering why Marion Faye, with whom she has also become involved after separating from Eitel, does not love her. Though Eitel returns to Desert D'Or to marry Elena following the accident, it is primarily out of guilt—something Elena no doubt senses, though she remains self-deprecating and uncertain. After the marriage and the birth of their child, Elena laments her lack of purpose, wondering out loud to Eitel, "What am I going to do with my life?" When he fails to respond, she apologizes for being a "bother" to him—the last line she utters in the novel (316).

In the end, we are left with only some of the characters living in a setting a notch above the "purgatorial." Marion, after recovering from the accident, is arrested and sent to jail. Eitel eventually submits to HUAC questioning and continues to make films with middling success and, though he is married to Elena, later takes up an affair with Lulu Meyers. Lulu and Teddy remained trapped in the Hollywood machine, with Teddy unable to come fully out of the closet. Sergius is the only one who seems to achieve some semblance of escape, traveling to Mexico, where he opens a bullfighting school and lives as a writer. However, as Barry Leeds has aptly noted, even though Sergius seems to embody some hope, "on both the individual and the societal levels it is a decidedly qualified hope" for "neither the Sergius nor the Eitel of the novel . . . succeed in being brave enough to make love work, and thereby to be saved."[26] In Leeds's view, this paves the way for Mailer to invent one of his best-known characters, a man who "will be brave enough" to make love work: Stephen Rojack in *An American Dream*. In addition to providing a springboard for this later character, Sergius, in his movement away from the life of Desert D'Or, also articulates what became a foundational aspect of Mailer's own worldview as expressed in both his fiction and his nonfiction: "There was that law of life so cruel and so just which demanded that one must grow or pay more for remaining the same" (294).

The Deer Park is an engrossing book at times—certainly closer to a "page turner" than *Barbary Shore*—and its social satire of Hollywood is biting and incisive. However, the novel received mixed reviews, and though Mailer took these in stride (defiantly placing the best and worst reviews side by side in advertisements for the book), the reception added to the stressful situation surrounding the novel's publication. *The Deer Park* was marked by a fraught compositional history, plagued by a controversy with Rinehart, Mailer's publisher. Rinehart was not pleased with the first two drafts of the novel, and Stanley Rinehart informed Mailer that he would have to omit "six not very explicit lines about the sex of an old producer and a call girl" in order for the book to be published.[27] While such a small passage might seem insignificant, Mailer's stubborn pride took hold, and as he himself notes, "The moment one was ready to consider losing those six lines they moved into the moral center of the novel."[28] When Mailer would not give in to Rinehart's demands, publication was halted, the contract ended, and the book went to eight publishing houses before finally being accepted at Putnam's. Mailer did end up making extensive revisions—though these were not demanded by an editor but propelled by his sense that the style and the voice of his narrator needed to be reworked sentence by sentence, changing "a poetic prose that was too self-consciously attractive and formal" to one that was more "rough" and "real," and had "a muscular body back of the voice."[29] Mailer would later note that *The Deer Park* was a more difficult book to write than *The Naked and the Dead*, and that he worked on the book in a "low mood."[30]

This dilemma and the criticism Mailer faced from various readers and editors while trying to get the book published, along with the poor reception of *Barbary Shore*, deeply affected him, and it would be years before he would write another novel. As he says retrospectively in *Advertisements for Myself*, "I was out of fashion and that was the score; that was all the score. . . . And so as the language of sentiment would have it, something broke in me, but I do not know if it was so much a loving heart as a cyst of the weak, the unreal, and the needy, and I was finally open to my anger" (234). Though Mailer notes that this anger eventually gave him the strength to fight for his work, it would take years for him to regain some of the confidence he lost during this period. Still, his experiences primed him for the work that was to come. "All I felt then," he says, "was that I was an outlaw, a psychic outlaw, and I liked it, I liked it a good night better than trying to be a gentleman. . . . for the first time in my life I knew what it was to make your kicks" (234). These revelations pave the way for some of his most interesting and controversial work to come in the 1950s and 1960s, and anticipate the public persona that would come to define him, for better or worse.

CHAPTER 3

An American Voice and *An American Dream*

After the controversy surrounding the publication of *The Deer Park,* Mailer took a hiatus from fiction; it would be nearly ten years before he would publish his next novel. Yet Mailer was by no means idle in the meantime, publishing a number of notable, influential, and at times provocative pieces during the ensuing decade. He contributed frequently to *Commentary, Dissent,* the *Village Voice,* and *Esquire,* well known and widely read for their editorial coverage of politics, cultural commentary, and current events. Mailer would later compile a number of these previously published pieces in three collections: *Advertisements for Myself* (1959), *The Presidential Papers* (1963), and *Cannibals and Christians* (1966), each of which provides an encapsulated view of Mailer's most passionate views and concerns while also offering insight into the public persona that he continued to shape during the late 1950s and into the 1960s.

In her review of *The Presidential Papers,* Midge Decter referred to the collection as "a public performance," an apt description, as it is in this period that Mailer firmly establishes himself as one of America's foremost public intellectuals, and one of its most prominent voices.[1] As Decter goes on to hypothesize: "Mailer's daring has to do with something not, I think, sufficiently taken into account about him, and for which *The Presidential Papers* brings massive evidence. And that is how *American* he is. By 'American' I do not mean anything literary-metaphysical. I mean quite simply that he owns America. He unquestioningly and unambiguously belongs here. . . . no one is currently telling us more about the United States of America."

This distinctly American nature of Mailer's writings in *The Presidential Papers* and elsewhere is particularly evident in the concern he demonstrates for the political and spiritual future of the nation. His investment in the vitality of American culture has the effect of linking what might otherwise be seen as a disparate range of topics; for instance, "Ten Thousand Words a Minute," his essay on the famous 1962 Floyd Patterson–Sonny Liston fight, says as much about America as his essay on John F. Kennedy's 1960 presidential campaign, "Superman Comes to the Supermarket," and perhaps even as much as his 1964 serialized novel, *An American Dream*. Indeed, Robert Solotaroff has called "Ten Thousand Words a Minute" the "nonfictional twin" of *An American Dream* since in both works Mailer "implicitly distinguishes between the white magic freed by self-reliance and the black magic invoked by swearing obedience to a sovereignty higher than oneself."[2] In each of these otherwise very different pieces, Mailer emphasizes the importance of individuality and self-reliance (foundational concepts of American identity) while pointing to the ways that conformity and obedience threaten to undermine such ideas, endangering the courage and creativity of the individual and the success of the nation.

Such concerns are noticeably present earlier, however, in 1959's *Advertisements for Myself*. This miscellany of excerpts and commentary marks the moment at which Mailer comes into his own as a public intellectual, and in which he debuts the incisively critical tone that came to define him as an imposing American voice in the ensuing years. Not only does this collection offer some of the first examples of Mailer's tendency to fashion himself as a character in his own creative nonfiction, but it also introduces many of Mailer's philosophies on gender, sexuality, violence, existential liberation, and politics in America. These theories later make their way into *An American Dream*, a work published relatively early in his career but which might be seen as a centerpiece of his oeuvre.

One of Mailer's key fixations in *Advertisements for Myself* is the figure of the "hipster." As Mailer explains, the "hipster" is the American existentialist who lives in "the undercurrents and underworlds of American life" among "the defeated, the isolated, the violent, the tortured, and the warped," and who rejects the oppressive conformity of American society (293). Mailer's theory of "Hip" is most famously laid out in his 1957 essay "The White Negro." Originally published in *Dissent* and reprinted in *Advertisements for Myself*, it has become a central, if problematic, part of Mailer's canon, serving as a foundation for the philosophies of existentialism, violence, masculinity, and social decay that Mailer would continue to revise and expand in ensuing decades. Specifically, the essay offers a theory of a new man of the future, one who would usher in an age of rebellion and liberation from social conformity and totalitarianism. This new "hipster" hero rejects everything that is "square"; he is an "urban frontiersman" in the romanticized tradition of the Wild West. He knows that to truly live, and to avoid "a slow death by conformity with every creative and rebellious instinct stifled," he must "divorce" himself from the totalitarian bounds of modern society, choosing instead to "exist without roots, to set out on that uncharted journey into the rebellious imperatives of the self."[3]

The hipster, in Mailer's theorization, is also an individual who can embrace the "psychopath" in himself. This notion of psychopathy is one of the more polemic tenets of Mailer's philosophy of "Hip," and one that draws connections between violence, masculine courage, and individual freedom that pervade many, if not most, of Mailer's works. As he posits in "The White Negro," the construction of the "psychopathic" hipster is founded on the idea that violence is often a necessary tool for liberation from a conformist society. To encourage one's inner psychopath is to embrace that violence as an inherent part of one's freedom: it is a rebellion against the institutional and actual violence of "the State," which Mailer believed was to blame for the gradual decay of individuality. Under circumstances in which civilization is built on a "cultureless and alienated bottom of exploitable human material," Mailer finds in violence creative potential and generative properties.[4] Violence is not only presented as essential to liberation from conformity but, in a seeming paradox, as a way to eradicate or diminish other violence; it is "a catharsis which prepares growth."[5] As Mailer explains, "The psychopath murders—if he has the courage—out of the necessity to purge his violence, for if he cannot empty his hatred then he cannot love, his being is frozen with implacable self-hatred for his cowardice" (320).

While compelling in certain respects, Mailer's theory of liberation is problematic because, at least in his early theorizing, it relies on the deployment of a violence that oppresses others, thus making any "liberation" possible only for the aggressor. Though Mailer would later address the consequences of interpersonal violence more fully, his comments during this period of his career are much more extreme, so much so as to seem almost sensationalist. In a 1955 *Village Voice* essay, for example, Mailer asserts that "to a Square, a rapist is a rapist. . . . But a hipster knows that the act of rape is a part of life too, and that even in the most brutal and unforgivable rape, there is artistry or the lack of it . . . and so no two rapists nor no two rapes are ever the same."[6] This suggestion that there are acceptable or "artistic" kinds of rape threatens to do irreparable damage to Mailer's theory by way of its moral relativism, and its apparent embrace of sexual and often gender-based, misogynistic violence. Indeed, the Hip "morality," which Mailer defines as "to do what one feels whenever and wherever it is possible" sounds suspiciously like *a*morality.[7] While Mailer's hipster might achieve a sense of freedom and catharsis from this act, it nevertheless comes at the expense of another whose freedom is suspended as a result.

Some additional controversy that arises from "The White Negro" has to do with its participation in long-held stereotypes about race, particularly its discussion of blackness. By imagining an ideal masculine figure who lives by what he calls a "black man's code," for instance, Mailer risks upholding racist stereotypes of the heightened sexuality and criminality often attributed to blackness. This element of Mailer's theory is founded on his belief that the black man exists in a type of liminal space in America, as "he has been living on the margin between totalitarianism and democracy for two centuries."[8] Because Mailer sees the black man in America through the lens of the stereotype perpetuated at the time—a hypersexualized, violent, criminalized figure—he views this figure as an ideal representative of the sexual and moral outlaw he envisions, a man "forced into the position of exploring all those moral wildernesses of civilized life which the Square automatically condemns as delinquent or evil or immature or morbid or self-destructive or corrupt."[9]

Through such language, Mailer maintains what James Baldwin later criticized as a mystique of black masculinity. In a 1961 article for *Esquire,* "The Black Boy Looks at the White Boy," Baldwin acknowledges that "to be an American Negro male is also be to be a kind of walking phallic symbol, which means that one pays, in one's own personality, for the sexual insecurity of others. The relationship, therefore, of a black boy to a white boy is a very complex thing."[10] It is this complexity to which Baldwin feels Mailer does not quite do justice, carrying the stereotype of the sexualized black man so far that "the *mystique* could only be extended into violence."[11] In other words, Baldwin accuses Mailer of perpetuating the myths that govern social assumptions about black masculinity, thus creating the "mystique" around the figure of the black man that further contributes to his otherness. In this way, one of the flaws with Mailer's fashioning of a masculine ethic defined by characteristics of an existential and violent outlaw is that, while the initial intention behind the representation of such a figure might be liberatory and equalizing, the means by which he achieves this goal threaten instead to reaffirm oppressive racial stereotypes.

At the same time, however, these effects must be reconciled in some way with the fact that these are the very kinds of assumptions and stereotypes that Mailer himself was initially attempting to eradicate. As Mailer stated forthrightly in a column for the *Village Voice* in 1956, "My passion . . . is to destroy stereotypes, categories, and labels."[12] Moreover, as he explained in *Dissent* in 1958, the "real desire" of the masculine figure he introduces in "The White Negro" is to "make a better world, one in which individual violence would "still spare us the collective violence of rational totalitarian liquidations" and "open the possibility of working with that human creativity which is violence's opposite."[13] The final vision Mailer holds is in fact one of "love" and "justice," in which all men are freed from their respective oppressions by the violence of the individual. Indeed, as J. Michael Lennon has pointed out in his biography of Mailer, despite the "vigorous rejoinders" inspired by the controversial passages in the essay, the work was also "celebrated for its orphic verve," and many readers recognized the essay for the "call to radical self-assertion" that it was intended to be, praising the work for its defiant and ultimately hopeful tone.[14] Nevertheless, Mailer leaves us with a series of contradictions that raise questions about the consequences of an individual violence that is both liberating and oppressive.

Despite the problematic reassertion of racial stereotypes in "The White Negro," Mailer does address and contest racism elsewhere in his writing. For instance, in *The Presidential Papers,* he comments not only on the unequal distribution of power along racial and ethnic lines, but on the internalization of inferiority experienced by minorities themselves. As he writes, "Minority groups are the artistic nerves of a republic, and like any phenomenon which has to do with art, they are profoundly divided. They are both themselves and the mirror of their culture as it reacts upon them. They are themselves and the negative truth of themselves. No white man, for example, can hate the Negro race with the same passionate hatred and detailed detestation that each Negro feels for himself and for his people; no anti-Semite can begin to comprehend the malicious analysis of his soul which every Jew indulges every day" (187).

This commentary, rather than threatening to perpetuate stereotypes, instead demonstrates an acute awareness of their implications, as Mailer observes the ways that various marginalized groups experience a self-loathing or engage in a "malicious analysis" of themselves that is sometimes more detrimental than the defamation they face at the hands of others. Mailer later clarifies in *Cannibals and Christians* that "a member of a minority group is—if we are to speak existentially—not a man who is a member of a category, a Negro or a Jew, but rather a man who feels his existence in a particular way"; in other words, "what characterizes a member of a minority group is that he is forced to see himself as both exceptional and insignificant, marvelous and awful, good and evil," and thus "by this definition nearly everyone in America is a member of a minority group, alienated from the self by a double sense of identity" (113–14). This statement, in addition to rethinking the centrality of marginalization in America, also exemplifies Mailer's ongoing interest in contradiction and his belief that America itself embodied numerous paradoxes. Indeed, most of his most interesting and complex protagonists in later works exhibit a struggle with the contradictory natures of their personalities and "a double sense of identity."

In his cultural commentary during this period, Mailer also continues to express his concern with conformity and the corruption fostered by politics and mass media. Often, he frames this discussion in terms of disease—thus, the recurring idea that a "plague" is consuming America manifests itself in a number of Mailer's works. These corruptions, in Mailer's mind, forced individuals to suppress their natural instincts and emotions, a situation that Mailer believed to be a cause of cancer—not only in the metaphorical sense of social decay, but also in the literal sense of physiological disease. In other words, the stress of repression would directly affect the cells of the body, causing them to mutate into cancerous cells (a theory that is not too distant from actual medical science, since we now know that emotional and psychological stress can manifest itself in a variety of physical ailments). In a speech prepared for a debate with William Buckley (also later published in *The Presidential Papers*), Mailer expounds on the metaphorical aspects of this discussion, expostulating on the plague that has fallen over America, which he believes is caused in large part by the political and social totalitarianism that pervades society. There, he states explicitly that "totalitarianism is better understood if it is regarded as a plague rather than examined as a style of ideology" and goes on to call it a "moral disease" (175) that in turn causes an "unspeakable illness of the psyche" (165).[15]

Mailer saw existentialism as an avenue for avoiding these cancer-causing oppressions and corruptions, arguing that an existential approach to life (which is itself a foundation of his theory of "Hip") would help individuals make more courageous decisions. As a result, they would live a life of action rather than one of passivity, a life of individualism and creativity rather than one of conformity. "Existential politics is simple," he writes. "It has a basic argument: if there is a strong ineradicable strain in human nature, one must not try to suppress it or anomaly, cancer, and plague will follow. Instead one must find an art into which it can grow."[16] The notion of growth is central to Mailer's idea of a more creative individual and a better world, and the metaphorical cancer imposed by totalitarian government, class structures, and even architecture inhibits such growth.

Moreover, in Mailer's view these totalitarian structures also threatened to advance a spiritual decay, both within the individual and within the nation at large. Concern for the soul is a deep and abiding preoccupation of Mailer's, and is directly connected to his belief in the power of existentialism. That is, existential courage was necessary for individual, spiritual growth. In a selection from *The Presidential Papers* called "On Dread," for example, he writes: "we feel anxiety because we are in danger of losing some part or quality of our soul unless we act, and act dangerously" (151).[17] In this way, Mailer's idea of an ongoing existential battle between God and the devil plays out on the individual level as well, the larger spiritual war manifesting itself in our personal battle to reject apathy and conformity and embrace change, creativity, and the unknown.

Mailer also saw existential violence as a natural and perhaps necessary response to the "cancer" of society. "Whenever people get collectively sick, the remedy becomes progressively more violent and hideous," he noted in a 1962 "Impolite Interview" with Paul Krassner. "An insidious, insipid sickness demands a violent far-reaching purgative."[18] In *Cannibals and Christians,* Mailer also writes, "There are souls which can be expressed—that is, undeadened—only by violence" (359). Throughout the 1950s and 1960s, Mailer continued to revise and rearticulate his evolving views on the role of violence as a marker of both masculine power and individual freedom. Though he frequently acknowledged his distaste for "inhuman" and "large scale" violence, his existential theories espoused in both his fiction and his nonfiction consistently suggest that he admired an individual violence that would allow one to move outside of the totalitarian structure of society.[19]

This theory of what Donald Kaufman calls "justifiable violence" also makes its way into Mailer's call for an existential hero who would help usher in an era of greater freedom and creativity.[20] In a section of *The Presidential Papers* titled "Heroes and Leaders," Mailer states directly: "Existential politics is rooted in the concept of the hero" (6), and "it is the unspoken thesis of these pages that no President can save America from a descent into totalitarianism without shifting the mind of the American politician to existential styles of political thought" (5). Mailer's ideal hero might more accurately be deemed an "outlaw hero"—someone who would break free of the strictures imposed by mainstream politicians, and in turn save the nation from what he referred to in "The White Negro" as a "slow death by conformity." Such a man would live on the margins of mainstream politics, and would introduce new and revolutionary ways of leading that would jolt America out of their conformist ennui and inaction.

This hope is embodied in one of Mailer's most famous essays, "Superman Comes to the Supermarket," originally published in *Esquire* and later collected in *The Presidential Papers.* This essay, which is often seen as Mailer's entrée into New Journalism, focuses on the potential of John F. Kennedy to lead America into a new and more promising era as the existential leader of a new age. Mailer argues that such an existential leader would "create a new reality" (26) and would work against what Mailer calls "the spirit of the supermarket, that homogenous extension of stainless surfaces and psychoanalyzed people, packaged commodities and ranch homes, interchangeable, geographically unrecognizable, that essence of the new postwar Super America" (32). Instead, he would embody the powerful American myth "that each of us was born to be free, to wander, to have adventure and to grow on the waves of the violent, the perfumed, and the unexpected" (39). This language exemplifies Mailer's indebtedness to the mythos of the western frontier, and the identity of the outlaw hero.[21] In *Cannibals and Christians* he reiterates this idea, noting that JFK's magnetism derives from the fact that "he offers us a mirror of ourselves, he is an existential hero, his end is unknown, it is even unpredictable, even as our end is unpredictable, and so in the time of crisis he is able to perform the indispensable psychic act of a leader, he takes our national anxiety so long buried and releases it to the surface—where it belongs" (216). Mailer's comments about the president's "unpredictable" and "unknown" end are eerily prescient, and Mailer felt the tragedy of JFK's assassination acutely, as his hopes for a new existential hero were snuffed out in an instant.

In fact, the impact of this event haunts many of Mailer's later works. Mailer captures the despair, fear, and uncertainty that defined American sentiment in the wake of this tragedy in a number of his ensuing publications, but perhaps nowhere more poignantly than in *An American Dream*. While a controversial novel, it is an example of some of Mailer's best writing. He himself proclaimed his belief that "sentence for sentence *An American Dream* is one of the better written books in the language," and many shared his enthusiasm for the book; upon its publication, Joan Didion raved that it was "the most serious New York novel since *The Great Gatsby*."[22] Published serially in *Esquire* from January through August 1964, and then published as a novel in 1965, the narrative grapples with themes of social decay, individual oppression, and violence via the existential quest of Stephen Rojack. As Frank McConnell argues, "*An American Dream*, in fact, takes the form of a mirror image of the Kennedy assassination. For if the nightmare forces of repressed violence were unleashed, against his will, against the radiantly successful Kennedy, Mailer gives us, in the fable of Rojack, a picture of an equally successful man's willing descent into the same spiritual maelstrom."[23] Yet Mailer does not resort to despair or nihilism in his exploration of such a descent; while Rojack's journey is winding, violent, and messy, the novel does offer a sense of hope. Though Mailer acknowledges the ways in which the American Dream has been compromised by political, corporate, and individual corruptions, all of which were punctuated by Kennedy's tragic death, his novel also demonstrates his belief in the possibility of redemption.

An American Dream distills many of the philosophical, political, and spiritual ideas that Mailer had been fashioning for the previous decade, and thus seems to be a natural extension of some of his nonfiction.[24] For instance, Nigel Leigh has argued that "'The White Negro' is an extremist celebration of libertarian values, an intoxicating and enabling piece of mythmaking; *An American Dream* is less reckless, an extended fictional exploration of some of its consequences" (87–88). The novel traces the journey of Stephen Rojack—war hero, professor of existential philosophy, commercially successful author, and well-known television personality—as he finds himself, as he says, at "the end of a very long street," having decided that he is "finally a failure" (8). As the narrative unfolds, Rojack embarks on an alcohol-soaked, sleepless, violent, and sex-filled bender, his behavior calling to mind the psychopathic hipster celebrated by Mailer in "The White Negro." Like that figure, Rojack acts on a desire for total freedom from the decaying, cancerous society he envisions around him. Feeling detached from the world he sees as oppressive to his individual freedom and the development of his masculine identity, he murders his wife, an act of violence that, in his mind, will free him from the suffocating class and social pressures he experiences. For Rojack, violence functions as a cleansing and cathartic force, its use justified by its potentially liberating end. Both the creative potential and the consequences of liberatory violence, then, become a key focus of *An American Dream*; in this way, Rojack's journey is a specific examination of the more abstract theory offered in "The White Negro."

Moreover, this violence is particularly connected to Mailer's definitions of masculinity. Early on, it becomes evident that tied up in this concept of violence are Rojack's conflicting perceptions of what it means to be a man; in fact, he seems able to discuss manhood *only* through the language of violence. Though he acknowledges that there "is something manly about containing your rage," murder "offers the promise of vast relief" and "exhilaration" (8). Thus, to be "manly" *inside* society, according to Rojack, is to repress one's instincts toward violence; to be manly *outside* of society—to live on the margins like Mailer's hypermasculine hipster—is to embrace these violent instincts. In either case, violence becomes the figure around which masculinity is fashioned, but it is the latter that Rojack wants to embody: that is, he wants to fashion a masculine identity founded on relief as opposed to restraint—for restraint is what causes the cancer that is destroying America.

The nuanced distinction between destructive and creative violence is a central theme of the novel. As a result, from the time of the novel's publication, many readers and critics have found difficulty coming to grips with its unsettling events and morally ambiguous antihero, consequently overlooking the novel's complexities in favor of a denunciation of its violence on moral and ethical grounds.[25] While it is important to question the ethical nature of violence in *An American Dream,* it is equally important to consider this violence as a literary trope, one that facilitates an analysis of Mailer's philosophies surrounding existential freedoms, social oppressions, and gendered relationships. Specifically, it draws attention to the ways that Mailer interrogates masculine anxiety, criticizes class hierarchy, and promotes the idea of redemptive love.

Rojack's relationship with his wife, Deborah, for example, is at the center of the novel's most unsettling passages but also informs the book's most salient themes. Deborah has helped Rojack fashion his current life of relative success and privilege, but because of this she also represents one of the many external threats to his manhood. Though Rojack looks back on the early years of their marriage with nostalgia, remembering Deborah's love for him as something that imbues him with "vitality," he also fears his own reliance on her; when they separate, for example, Rojack admits, "all of my substance fell out of me" (18). Rojack attributes Deborah's influence to a feminine mysticism that would supposedly afford her the ability to "lay a curse" on him should she choose to do so (22). This, coupled with his depiction of her as a "Great Bitch" who "delivers extermination to any bucko brave enough to take carnal knowledge of her" appears to be Rojack's suggestion that he would be justified in defending himself against her cruelties; it is an attempt to prematurely excuse his murder of her (9). Living with Deborah, for example, Rojack admits he was "murderous," but also acknowledges that Deborah herself "was not incapable of murdering" him herself (9).

While it has opened up Mailer's text to accusations of misogyny, this depiction of Deborah also brings to light the fact that Rojack's own sense of compromised masculinity and his use of violence are not entirely a result of his fear of women (though that comes into play here), but also a result of his reliance on the hierarchical and limiting class structures of society that seem to dictate the status of his manhood. His sense of inferiority in the face of his wife is augmented by his awareness that his success has largely been a result of her social connections. "She had been my entry into the big league," he explains. "I had loved her with the fury of my ego, that way I loved her still, but I loved her the way a drum majorette loved the power of the band for the swell it gave to each little strut" (17). His love for her, as he himself realizes, is based on her ability to build him up, to support him, and to feed his ego by introducing him into the upper echelons of society—and it is society that Rojack feels to be his true enemy. In other words, Mailer's aim here is not to fashion a masculine hero whose primary aim is to exert control over Deborah—or over women in general—but one whose aim is to free himself from the socially imposed obligation to abide by this gender hierarchy at all.

However, this freedom comes not only at the expense of Deborah's freedom but her life, which makes a justification of violence difficult to digest: in stark, visceral and grotesque detail and in crisp, straightforward prose, Mailer recounts the way Rojack "struck her a blow on the back of the neck, a dead cold chop which dropped her to a knee, and then hooked an arm about her head and put a pressure on her throat" (30). The brief description of Deborah's murder is saturated with details that lay the foundation for Mailer's representation of a liberating power of violence that emphasizes catharsis and rebirth, wherein a new beginning outside of the previous confines of his life seems possible. Rojack's own reflections as he kills Deborah reference a transcendent "crossing over" and suggest an emergence into a new and better existence. As he strangles Deborah, he feels hatred pass from him in "wave after wave," and is driven to continue by the promise of some beauty—images of "jeweled cities" and a "tropical dusk"—that exist beyond this door and seem to represent recompense for his actions upon their completion. This vision of a remunerative paradise is supplemented by Rojack's sense that all of his hatred and illness depart upon his passage through the door—in fact, the language suggests that Rojack is describing his own death experience. This metaphorical death is followed closely by his metaphorical rebirth, for after he commits the murder, he feels that he sees the world with new eyes; every detail is fascinating, clear, and exhilarating. By subverting the horrific detail and foregrounding the euphoric sensations of his protagonist, Mailer treats the act of murder as a triumph over decay and corruption, imbuing Rojack with "faith in the creative possibilities of the human being to envisage acts of violence as the catharsis which prepares growth"—evocative of the "psychopathic hipster" who murders "out of the necessity to purge his violence, for if he cannot empty his hatred then he cannot love."

The aftermath of the murder, despite its emphasis on transcendence, is equally disconcerting, since Rojack appears to resume his daily routine without difficulty or guilt; everything he does is presented as mundane in the face of what seems a so decidedly abnormal and horrifying act. Yet one could argue this effect is deliberate, as it does not diminish the horrifying nature of murder itself; in fact, the juxtaposition between the systematic details of Deborah's murder and Rojack's spiritual rebirth is *meant* to be unsettling, and we are not meant to see violence as purely triumphant. Moreover, while Rojack is not brought to justice under the law, his actions do not go unquestioned or uncriticized within the construct of the narrative. After the murder, for example, Rojack has not achieved the freedom he seeks—either from Deborah or his attachments to society. This is suggested by another disturbing moment in the aftermath of the murder. When Rojack finally returns to Deborah's body to consider his plan of action, he finds himself overcome with rage again, feeling "an impulse to go up to her and kick her ribs, grind my heel on her nose, drive the point of my shoe into her temple and kill her again, kill her good this time, kill her right" (50). This violent desire is also accompanied by a strange cannibalistic fantasy in which he places Deborah's body in the bathtub to "sup on [her] flesh," for in this way he feels he might be able to "digest [his] wife's curse before it could form" (50).

While some might (and indeed, have) read such a scene as evidence of the novel's potentially misogynistic undertones, there is another, equally viable, way to interpret this scene. Rojack's impulse suggests that even in her death Deborah seems to exert an influence over him, diminishing his power and instilling fear within him, as if to prove his impulse toward masculine dominance is destined to be unsuccessful. Tied to gendered stereotypes that have been instilled within him by society, Rojack maintains his belief in a mystical power that Deborah might be able to wield over him from the grave and is therefore not, in fact, entirely free from his gendered anxiety. Moreover, as Rojack begins to envision the potential consequences of his actions, he realizes that his violent method of freeing himself of his wife may actually be his undoing and that he has not been truly freed.

A similar apprehension also manifests itself within Rojack's ensuing relationship with Cherry Melanie, a romance that is meant to indicate his ability to love after purging his hatred through violence. With Cherry, however, as with Deborah, Rojack reveals an anxiety that arises from the threat of female power. As Rojack watches Cherry sing in a nightclub on the day they meet, he surmises in a drunken haze that "women must murder us unless we possess them altogether," and admits to having a "fear" of Cherry that can only be resolved by his attempt to possess her; immediately thereafter, he imagines himself shooting an arrow into her womb (100). Initially, this imagined violence seems to clearly embody Rojack's patriarchal aim to establish control over Cherry, by way of his ability to inflict damage on the source of Cherry's own (biologically) creative power. Yet Mailer also imbues Rojack with regret over this action. Soon after this illusory act of violence, Rojack pictures himself "draining poison from the wound" he had imaginatively inflicted, after which he himself becomes sick, as though he is purging the violence from the both of them (101). Thus, immediately after he envisions exacting violence upon Cherry, Rojack not only assumes responsibility for it, but imposes it upon himself. These contradictory impulses to both harm Cherry and to save her reflect Rojack's similarly conflicted desire to love Cherry even as he feels threatened by her. "Let me love that girl, and become a father, and try to be a good man, and do some decent work," Rojack prays at one point (162). And indeed, though she cannot offer the justification for violence that he seeks, and though Rojack's prayers here are not quite answered, Cherry will ultimately offer Rojack at least the chance, in his mind, for redemption.

Rojack's interaction with Shago Martin, a well-known jazz artist (modeled after Miles Davis) and Cherry's ex-boyfriend offers yet another episode within which Mailer is able to both endorse and question violent masculine empowerment.[26] Shago immediately poses a threat to Rojack not only because he is in competition for Cherry, but also because he represents the powerful and sexually potent male "other" who, in his powerful evocation of the figure depicted in "The White Negro," challenges Rojack's sense of manhood. In fact, Laura Adams has argued that Shago is the figure mythologized in that earlier essay, a logical assumption, as the description of both Shago's music and appearance largely mimics that of Mailer's "hipster."[27] As Rojack explains, for example, Shago "had a beat which went right through your ear into your body, it was cruel, it was perfect" (182), an assessment that echoes Mailer's discussion of the role of jazz in his hipster ideology and its similar ability to infiltrate the body through its "knifelike entrance into culture, its subtle but so penetrating influence."[28] Moreover, Shago's music sounds like a "clash of hysterias" (183), much as the Hip philosophy articulated by Mailer in "The White Negro" was meant to usher in an age of "new hysteria."[29] This, for Rojack, is yet another significant point that feeds his admiration, as Shago thus seems to have broken through the social conformity he finds suffocating and to have introduced something entirely new, strange, and unsettling.

Mailer's depiction of Shago, however, not only reaffirms but also revises Rojack's perceptions of blackness as a model of hypermasculinity, prompting Rojack to briefly reconsider his own mythologizing of race and gender. While the scene reasserts certain racialized stereotypes of gender, it also points to a mutual identification between Rojack and Shago. Rojack remembers, for example, that when he had seen Shago's face before on record covers and on film, he had decided it was "a handsome face, thin and arrogant," but also, clearly, "a mask" (180). His sense that Shago dons a performative guise for the public demonstrates his awareness that there might be a disconnect between the appearance Shago puts forth—the confident, sexual, fast-talking bastion of black masculinity—and the identity behind the mask, one that, in fact, will prove to be much more vulnerable. This also opens up the possibility for Rojack to identify with Shago: as he senses Shago's human vulnerability, Rojack begins to search for commonality between the two men. However, the common ground that Rojack begins to locate with Shago ultimately only reinforces his emphasis on violence as a sign of masculine power. Rojack senses a connection between himself and Shago, yet his feeling of "curious happiness" about this identification arises from "the knowledge Shago was capable of murder" (183). Thus, while a shared capacity to commit murder draws the two men together, it also increases the tension between them.

While the physical fight that ensues demonstrates a shared masculine anxiety between the two men grounded in a reciprocity of fear and desire, it also serves as a means for Rojack to attempt to appropriate those qualities he feels he is lacking by overcoming Shago with physical force. And indeed, before Rojack throws Shago down the stairs in his final triumphant move of the fight, he notes that "violence seemed to shake itself free from [Shago] every time I smashed him back to the floor and shake itself into me" (193). As with his murder of Deborah and his metaphorical wounding of Cherry, Rojack imagines that he can take another's power into himself through his own act of violence.[30] However, after he sees Shago leave Cherry's apartment, he is suddenly overwhelmed with dread; as after the murder of Deborah, his euphoria is only temporary. "It had all gone wrong again," he says. "If I could have taken some of it back, I would have returned to that moment when I began to beat Shago to the floor and he dared me to let him go" (195). In retrospect, he also senses that his actions have done irreparable damage to his relationship with Cherry, and that, because of this fight, "some flaw would continue to rot at the center" of their bond (199).

This embedded ambivalence about the intersections between violence, masculine identity, and liberation is also present in Rojack's climactic meeting with Barney Oswald Kelly, Deborah's father. If the novel has a villain, it is Kelly, framed here as the face of corporate America. Despite Kennedy's place in the novel, the middle name "Oswald" was not a deliberate reference to Lee Harvey Oswald—as Mailer says in *Cannibals and Christians*, he began working on *An American Dream* two months before the Kennedy assassination. However, as Mailer also notes of this happenstance, "If psychic coincidences give pleasure to some I do not know if they give them to me."[31] Nevertheless, the coincidental naming does help to further Mailer's representation of Kelly as a corrupting force of America, one that Rojack pits himself against. After Kelly confesses to Rojack that he had also been involved sexually with Cherry, Rojack prepares to fight—but this time, he balks at his own potential use of violence and instead decides that a real test of his masculine courage would be to walk around the parapet of Kelly's building. This is the third time Rojack will have attempted this feat in the novel, yet this moment is marked by his belief that, if he should successfully complete a trip around the walls of the tower, he will be released from the guilt of murdering Deborah and injuring Shago, and will thus be free embark on a new life with Cherry.

Yet Rojack cannot be absolved from this guilt: in a tragic twist, he returns to Harlem after circling the parapet to discover that Cherry is dying, fatally beaten by a member of Shago's gang—a conclusion that punctuates the paradoxical nature of violence that has pervaded the novel.In one sense, Cherry's death does serve to release Rojack from his last attachment to society, thus affording him the opportunity to escape; he retreats to the desert and strikes out on his own, ultimately living the life of the outsider he desired, considering himself part of the "new breed" of man being fashioned in the West (269).In this way, Mailer appears to uphold the concept of violence as a successful tool for liberation and masculine power by allowing Rojack the escape he wants, and his conclusion seems determined to justify Rojack's actions by inviting us to accept violence as an inherent characteristic of individual life and an embedded characteristic of modern culture. Indeed, Daniel Fuchs has recently argued that in *An American Dream,* "we have murder without consequences, crime without punishment," a statement reminiscent of Kate Millett's accusation in *Sexual Politics* that Mailer allows his protagonist to get away with murder, and such interpretations make sense upon a superficial reading of the novel's conclusion.[32]

These assertions, however, do not quite do justice to Mailer's dialectical treatment of violence. That is, Mailer seems equally determined to demonstrate the ways that Rojack's quest is unsuccessful, by emphasizing that his murder of Deborah has set in motion a chain of events that have led directly to Cherry's own death, thus ruining his chance at redemptive love. Of course, the fact that Rojack survives while Deborah and Cherry must die seems cruelly unjust—but that is precisely Mailer's point. Though Rojack can escape to the desert and face no legal penalty for his violence, to a certain degree Mailer himself recognizes that the justice in—and justification for—his violence must be called into question. As Mailer stated in a 1961 interview, "Violence must be violence for which full responsibility is accepted, and that's rare today. Today we have the violence of the man who won't look his victim in the face" (66).[33]

The alternating venerations and criticisms of violence in *An American Dream* highlight the way Mailer struggled to acknowledge the victims of violence within his fiction while also incorporating violence into his model for a liberated man of the future. The novel's complex depiction of violence, along with Mailer's ability to make his murderous protagonist a sympathetic character even until the end, has led to a wide range of critical conclusions. For Barry Leeds, Rojack ultimately "comes to represent what Mailer perceived as most idealistic and courageous in the American national character, what became corrupted by compromise with a venal society, and what may ultimately be redeemed through courage, discipline and selfless, procreative love."[34] By contrast, for Bob Batchelor, the "moral" of the story is much darker. As he writes, Mailer's American Dream is funneled through Rojack as a nightmare bordering on madness, which then exposes how depraved the nation has grown.[35] These alternate interpretations tap into the very heart of Mailer's work in general, which so often straddles the line between light and dark, good and evil. Mailer continued to struggle with his own view of America in this context, examining its corruptions, idiosyncrasies, and values in his political writings during the late 1960s and early 1970s.

CHAPTER 4

Mailer on War, Women, Politics, and Film

Though Mailer had been deeply concerned with and involved in American politics from the start of his career, his involvement accelerated in the late 1960s and into the 1970s. This was an incredibly prolific period for Mailer: in a span of only five years, he produced one novel (*Why Are We in Vietnam?*), six nonfiction books (*The Armies of the Night, Miami and the Siege of Chicago, Of a Fire on the Moon, The Prisoner of Sex, St. George and the Godfather,* and *Existential Errands*), and three experimental films (*Wild 90, Beyond the Law,* and *Maidstone*). He also made numerous public appearances and frequently engaged in dialogues with the burgeoning second-wave feminist movement (most notably in a 1971 public debate now widely known as "Town Bloody Hall"), and somehow, amid all of this, he managed to launch a brief but much-publicized New York City mayoral run.

While all of this activity contributed to Mailer's ongoing role as one of America's foremost public intellectuals, his nonfiction published during this time has garnered him the most acclaim—even though Mailer considered much of his nonfiction to be secondary to his novels. In a 2007 interview for the *The Paris Review,* Mailer stated that he had "often been happy writing nonfiction because it's easier than writing novels" since "you don't have to worry about the story," and noted that he simply "wrote nonfiction because the jobs were offered to me."[1] This relative dismissal, though, does not reflect the impact of works like *The Armies of the Night,* Mailer's Pulitzer Prize–winning account of the 1967 march on the Pentagon, and *Miami and the Siege of Chicago,* his narrative of the national Republican and Democratic conventions of 1968. In both of these books, Mailer successfully captures the divisive and chaotic nature of American politics in the 1960s, offering thoughtful but incisive cultural and political criticism through his unique blend of literary journalism and historical narrative.

In *The Armies of the Night* (1968), Mailer becomes both observer and protagonist in his nonfictional narrative, adding an emotional investment and dramatic flair to his chronicle of events. This marks the first of many instances in which Mailer employed "illeism," the process of referring to himself in the third person, thus blurring the already muddy divisions between author, narrator, and character. Mailer himself acknowledges the problematic implications of such a style, admitting, "To write an intimate history of an event which places its focus on a central figure who is not central to the event, is to inspire immediate questions about the competence of the historian" (67).[2] However, as he also notes, "for this historian, there is no other choice. . . . The March on the Pentagon was an ambiguous event" so "an eyewitness who is a participant but not a vested partisan is required" (67). In other words, Mailer believes he must write subjectively as opposed to objectively to capture the nuances and ambiguities of the event. To write a straightforward piece would be misleading, for to represent the event as a series of undisputed facts would be to overlook its complexities, since the sentiments of those involved ranged from ambivalence to passionate anger. Moreover, as Jason Mosser has noted, "Mailer's focus on his own perceptions and impressions does at times intensify the reader's consciousness in sympathetic union with the narrator's," thus inviting the reader into the narrative in more complex ways.[3]

Mailer's own description of himself in *Armies* as "an eyewitness who is a participant but not a vested partisan" is apt, for it becomes evident that he is of two minds about the execution of the affair. On principle, he is against the war in Vietnam and thus ideologically supports the protest. As he writes, "Certainly any war was a bad war which required an inability to reason as the price of retaining one's patriotism; finally any war which offered no prospect of improving itself as a war—so complex and compromised were its roots—was a bad war" (208). Yet it is important to remember that here we have an older and wiser Mailer than the man who wrote passionate but problematic essays ten years earlier in *Advertisements for Myself.* The Mailer of 1968 looks upon the current generation of young people involved in the march with a hopeful but skeptical eye, recognizing the occasionally blind passion the protesters exhibit. "Like a later generation which was to burn holes in their brain on Speed, he had given his own head the texture of a fine Swiss cheese," he admits. "It had given him the illusion he was a genius, as indeed an entire generation of children would so come to see themselves a decade later out on celestial journeys of LSD" (15). This bemused appraisal—about the protest, about the mindset and lifestyle of the generation behind it—runs throughout the narrative, as Mailer feels a distinct disconnect from the crowd's generally myopic passion. Though he felt exhilarated and ultimately invigorated by his (brief) incarceration for protesting the war, his is a more tempered kind of passion here.[4]

Moreover, while he is as candid about his ego as ever (he admits he had been "boycotting" National Book Award events for some time and "thought it was the least he could do" in protest of the fact that his books had not as of yet been nominated), his tempered passion also translates into a more prominent humility (17). As he says of himself, "Boldness, attacks of shyness, rude assertion, and circumlocutions tortured as arthritic fingers working at lace, all took their turn with him, and these shuttlings of mood became most pronounced in their resemblance to the banging and shunting of freight cars when he was with liberal academics" (28). As a result, he is also very aware of the image he is presenting, and admits as much. "He had in fact learned to live in the sarcophagus of his image—at night, in his sleep, he might dart out, and paint improvements on the sarcophagus," he says (15–16). This observation exemplifies Mailer's acute awareness of the split identities that result from making his life a commodity for public consumption. As Jonathan D'Amore has noted, implicit in Mailer's remark that he lives in the "sarcophagus" of his own image "is the belief that inside one's image is a living, breathing, private person, and explicit in it is the concept of one's public image as a container for a private life ended, a deceased individual."[5]

The first part of *Armies* is, then, as much about Mailer's public image as it is about the march itself. The day prior to the march, Mailer recounts in detail the hours leading up to his stint as master of ceremonies at the Ambassador Theater, where a crowd has gathered to hear from Robert Lowell and Dwight Macdonald. Exhilarated, he claims to be "feeling the high sense of clarity which accompanies the light show of the aurora borealis when it is projected upon the inner universe of the chest, the lungs, and the heart" (40). He is also fairly drunk and proceeds to deliver a series of puzzling remarks in a southern accent, to which the crowd responds variously, some confused, some encouraging, some disparaging. (Someone calls him a "publicity hound," to which Mailer responds simply, "Fuck you.") Mailer incurs the disapproval of the organizers, and is not asked to speak the next day.

Moreover, prior to giving his introduction, his intoxication prompts him to urinate on the floor of the men's room. In a humorous move, though, Mailer lends nearly as much linguistic gravitas to this moment as he does to the march itself. As he writes, for example: "Master of Ceremonies breathes deep of the great reveries of this utterly non-Sisyphian release—at last!!—and thoroughly enjoyed the next forty-five seconds, being left on the aftermath not a note depressed by the condition of the premises. No, he was off on the Romantic's great military dream, which is: seize defeat, convert it to triumph" (43).

His reflections on the march itself, however, are more seriously introspective. Mailer is moved by the symbolic nature of the event, just as he is disturbed by the symbolic nature of the Pentagon toward which they are marching in protest. He observes the "floods of totalitarian architecture, totalitarian superhighways, totalitarian smog, totalitarian food (yes, frozen), totalitarian communications" (199) and calls the Pentagon the embodiment of this totalitarianism, a "blind five-sided eye of a subtle oppression which had come to America out of the very air of the country" (135). Yet while "there was probably no impotence in all the world like knowing you were right and the wave of the world was wrong" (199), Mailer finds some disappointment in the execution of the event: for example, the drama of the march is somewhat dissipated by the fact that the Pentagon is not fully visible since the parking lot is so expansive (in itself an example of the kind of totalitarian architecture Mailer hated). Nevertheless, he muses: "The air between New York and Washington was orgiastic with the breath of release, some promise of peace and new war seemed riding the phosphorescent wake of this second and last day's siege of the Pentagon, as if the country were opening into more and more on the resonance of these two days, more that was good, more that was bad" (240).

The second, briefer part of *Armies* is titled "The Novel as History," and here Mailer narrates from a more detached perspective—he is "the Historian" rather than "the Novelist." In this section, he explores the logistics and planning of the march, explaining the planning committee's reconnaissance of the Pentagon, and marveling that "it is not even a building one needs a pass to enter, and on an average working day no guards are visible"—something that might seem unfathomable to a post-9/11 reader (253). As he further states, "they could even if they had wished probably have paid a call on the Secretary of Defense to inform him of their project, yet it was impossible to locate the symbolic loins of the building—paradigm of the modern world indeed, they could explore every inch of their foe and know nothing about him" (255). In other words, Mailer locates another paradox: the building appears easily accessible, and citizens are free to enter, though once there they discover the labyrinthine structure of the building, and what seemed comprehensible and approachable is in fact unknowable.

Of further frustration to Mailer is his suspicion that the march is perhaps *too* polite, and as a result will fail to have truly meaningful impact. The event itself, he believes, had become a kind of compromise, which "said in effect: we, the government, wage the war in Vietnam for our security, but will permit your protest provided it is only a little disorderly. The demonstrators: we still consider the war outrageous and will therefore break the law, but not by very much" (268). This, coupled with an increasing impression of the power and presence of totalitarian structures and government, prompts Mailer to return to his metaphor of disease to describe the country, urging his readers to reflect upon an America that was "once a beauty of magnificence unparalleled, now a beauty with leprous skin" (320). In a line that echoes Yeats's worried question in "The Second Coming"—"And what rough beast, its hour come round at last / Slouches toward Bethlehem to be born?"—Mailer too wonders what America's "fearsome labor" will bring. "She will probably give birth, and to what?—the most fearsome totalitarianism the world has ever known?" (320).

Still, Mailer has not given up on the promise of America's unparalleled beauty. As a member of the front lines during the march, he maintains his position, crosses a roped line guarded by military police, is subsequently arrested, and spends a night in jail in order to fight for the freedoms he still believes are possible to attain in America. He still holds out hope—more than Yeats would allow in his own musings on an impending cultural shift fifty years prior. For Mailer, America still has the potential to "deliver a babe of a new world brave and tender, artful and wild," and so calls his readers to "end on the road to that mystery courage, death, and the dream of love give promise of sleep" (320).

The Armies of the Night was not the only vehicle for Mailer's criticisms of America in the 1960s, particularly the country's role in Vietnam. In 1967, the year prior to his march on the Pentagon, Mailer penned the novel *Why Are We in Vietnam?* which follows D.J. (the narrator), his father Rusty, and his friend Tex as they embark on a guided hunting trip to Alaska. Nominated for a National Book Award, the novel is notable for its vivid descriptions of the Alaskan wilderness, its use of an unreliable narrator (who himself calls attention to this unreliability and shifting identity throughout the novel), and for its use of obscenity-laced, stream-of-consciousness style which, like much of Mailer's experimental styles, polarized many readers.

Despite the book's title, the war in Vietnam is only directly mentioned once, in the last paragraph of the novel, but the narrative can nevertheless be seen as an allegory for the mentality that led the country into the quagmire of Vietnam. More specifically, an extended and indirect answer to the question posed in the title can be found in the novel's interrogation of its protagonists, with the aggressive, hypermasculine behavior of the characters symbolizing the hawkish American attitudes that left the military mired in an unwinnable war. In a letter to Walter Minton at Putnam in 1967, Mailer himself summarized this aim, instructing Minton to convey in the book's press materials that "Norman Mailer is saying, 'This perhaps is what we Americans are like, and this may be one of the reasons we're engaged in such a war.'"[6]

While many critics have acknowledged this allegory, Richard Fulgham has provided one of the most astute interpretations of the novel's intentions, also speaking to the underlying criticisms of traditional masculine behavior. As he observes, in *Vietnam,* "Mailer is blaming our presence in Southeast Asia on the collective heart of the hunter" and is also offering an "intentional parody of Hemingway's claim that killing a big animal was somehow noble."[7] In this way, the novel can be seen as an investigation of the rites and expectations of manhood, particularly the notion that masculinity is conferred by violence (an idea that Mailer explores in many of his works, including *An American Dream*). For example, while on the Alaskan hunting trip with his father, D.J. himself seems to embrace, at least to an extent, the idea that deploying violence and "animal murder" will imbue him with a specifically masculine power. At one point, when he and Tex are watching two grizzly bears in the wild, D.J says he'd "kiss LBJ on the petoons just to have a rifle to take down Griz 2 and see how he look when he die" (193). He recognizes the power and respect such an act would confer upon him. Yet he is also very aware of the kind of masculine stereotype he is embracing, explaining (while referring to himself in the third person) that "D.J. suffers from one great American virtue, or maybe it's a disease or ocular dysfunction—D.J. sees right through shit" (49).

Thus D.J. can see through the veneer of the hunting trip to what it is at its core: "ego status embroilments between numbers, guides, and executives" (49). As D.J. also knows, everyone on the hunting trip, including the guides and his own father, "has the sexual peculiarities of red-blooded men, which is to say that one of them can't come unless he's squinting down a gunsight, and the other won't produce unless his wife sticks a pistol up his ass" (12). This blunt admission, which suggests manhood and virility are conferred by way of violence, draws attention to the absurdity of such constructions of manhood.

Moreover, Rusty's obsession with killing a bear (as opposed to a rabbit or a caribou, far less impressive prey in his eyes) in order to prove his manhood to the group is portrayed as pathetic, as opposed to courageous or admirable. Without a bear, D.J. tells us, "Rusty and his status . . . can now take a double pine box funeral" (55). What Rusty fails to see is that there's a "fucking nervous system running through the earth and air of this whole State of Alaska, and the bear is tuned in . . . and the air, man, the air is the medium and the medium is the message, that Alaska air is real message—it says don't bullshit, buster" (54). Rusty is all "bullshit," all performance, concerned only with how he is perceived, lacking any connection to the intensity of what is around him; this, Mailer seems to suggest, is where American masculinity is headed, for Rusty is "corporation, right, that means he's a voice" (51). Even D.J., who "sees through shit," succumbs to the kind of destructive violence that has come to define

America and the American man, as he too goes off to Vietnam and commits violence of the "soldierest sort."

While for most of the narrative D.J. and Tex are full of the kind of confidence that is often integral to definitions of American masculinity, when they go out alone in the wilderness to camp, without weapons or gear, "awe and Dread is up on their back clawing away like a cat because they *alone,* man, you dig?" (187). When D.J. sees the "colors began to go from snow gold and yellow to rose and blue, coral in the folds of the ridges when the sun still hit, coral bright as the underside of the horn of the Dall ram" (195), he feels "full of beauty" (196). Despite the somewhat pessimistic ending of the novel, which sees D.J. go off to Vietnam to presumably (if temporarily) embrace the identity of the aggressive masculine soldier, here he has a moment of clarity. He realizes what Rusty failed to realize: that the world is bigger than his gendered anxiety, and that his own need to prove his manhood in the wilderness seems petty and inauthentic when actually confronted with that wilderness.

The novel's design, however, obfuscates this message for many readers. The book is written in a stream-of-consciousness style, with D.J. moving back and forth between first-person (in the "Intro Beeps" that precede each chapter) and third-person narration (within the chapters themselves). The chaos that results from this back and forth led Robert Solotaroff to describe D.J. as "a human amplifier for the madness of America."[8] D.J. himself is an unreliable narrator—in fact, in a Modernist self-reflexive manner, he draws attention to his own unreliability. For example, after what he calls his "Intro Beep" at the beginning of the novel (meant to mimic a radio transmission), he says to the reader, "The fact of the matter is that you're up tight with a mystery, me, and this mystery can't be solved because I'm the center of it and I don't comprehend, not necessarily, I could be traducing myself" (23). The particular way he "traduces" himself is by suggesting that he might not, in fact, be D.J., a privileged young white man from Texas, but might instead be a black man in Harlem, narrating the tale through the jive-inflected language of the hipster. "Maybe all of this humor here is absolute pretense," he goes on to say. "Or maybe I'm a Spade and writing like a Shade" (26). By prefacing the book in a way that invites the reader to be skeptical of the authority and identity of the narrator, Mailer also invites us to question how much of D.J.'s narrative is rhetoric, exaggeration, bombast, or performance. The novel's irony and self-reflexivity, expressed directly through D.J., lays the foundation for an assessment of aggressive masculine performance. With this in mind, the reader sees that D.J.'s descriptions of Rusty and of himself (as he goes off to war with an anticipatory "Vietnam, hot damn") imply that both men, despite their different ways of seeing, have bought into a "front." Thus, reflecting his own preoccupation with a certain existential notion of violent masculine identity, Mailer is courting uncertainty, using D.J. to question whether there might be any idea of "true manhood" at all.

An additional obstacle to widespread appreciation of this novel is its obscenity-laced language, which many readers found offensive, off-putting, or simply unnecessary.[9] Yet this obscenity is not simply present for shock value: for Mailer, it has deep and abiding meaning for America; indeed, Eliot Fremont-Smith has said that the language of this novel suggests that Mailer is not his generation's Hemingway, but its Swift.[10] As Mailer would later say in *The Armies of the Night,* "the noble common man was as obscene as an old goat, and his obscenity was what saved him. The sanity of said common democratic man was in his humor, and his humor was in his obscenity" (61). In *Vietnam,* this humorous obscenity has the potential to be a saving grace because it invites us to read between the lines, prompting us to avoid the complacent conformity that Mailer believed contributed to the decay of American society. The uncomfortable laughter that arises from the obscenity allows us to see what is amusing, misguided, ironic, or aberrant about human behavior, and thus stimulates our critical faculties. The language pushes us to read in a way we might not otherwise; moreover, it pushes us to question norms—particularly those that define the parameters of masculine identity—rather than to simply accept them as infallible truths. Mailer believed constant questioning, argument, creativity, and critical thinking would save America; hence his remark in *Armies* that in obscenity there was "no villainy" but only "his love for America" (60).

Why Are We In Vietnam? also marks a moment during which Mailer was experimenting more heavily with what might be termed the "avant-garde" in his work.[11] This is even more evident in his foray into film the ensuing year. After devoting so much time to his writing and to his work on a stage adaptation of *The Deer Park,* Mailer was excited to work in a new medium, which he believed would allow him to probe the depths of the human psyche in new ways. "Film speaks to the lost islands of the mind," he writes in his essay, "A Course in Filmmaking," and it "lives somewhere in that underground river of the psyche which travels from the domain of sex through the deeps of memory and the dream."[12] This was not Mailer's first foray into the world of filmmaking. Much earlier in his career, he and Jean Malaquais had spent time in Hollywood working on a film adaptation of Nathanael West's *Miss Lonelyhearts.* Though he and Malaquais were great friends, they soon discovered they did not work well together in this capacity. They failed to produce a complete script in time and were soon fired by Sam Goldwyn (though Mailer would later say that he quit "one minute before he was fired"). As Mailer recounts in an interview with Michael Chaiken, "Hollywood for me was a failure. A total failure, though I guess what stayed with me was this idea of making movies."[13]

The three films to which he devoted so much of his attention and personal finances—*Wild 90, Beyond the Law,* and *Maidstone*—exemplify the kind of ambitious experimentation that defines so much of Mailer's career. None of these films contains what could be considered a straightforward narrative; rather, Mailer instructed his actors to improvise around a theme while he let the camera run, later editing together hours of footage to create a more constrained piece. *Wild 90* and *Beyond the Law,* both filmed in 1967, are shot in black and white, a combined homage to a campy old-fashioned gangster film and Modernist self-reflexivity. *Wild 90* is an improvisational film about three "gangsters" (played by Mailer, Mickey Knox, and Buzz Farbar), all holed up together in a room "for various vague reasons." The camera follows them around as they try to fill the long hours trapped together in a confined space by drinking, insulting one another, cleaning their guns, and enjoying visits from girlfriends and acquaintances. The unscripted film was released to mixed reviews, alienating many viewers as a result of its seemingly aimless dialogue and its poor sound quality, a result of an on-set technical error that prompted cinematographer D. A. Pennebaker to beg Mailer not to release the film, and which led Mailer to remark that the film sounds "like everybody is talking through a jock strap."[14]

Though the film is raw and flawed in a number of ways, it is interesting for its self-referential nature—particularly, its send-up of the kind of machismo that it represents. This is particularly evident in the character of Prince, played by Mailer, who enacts the most drunken bravado of the three main characters. Prince stomps around, pushing over chairs and kicking boxes; he shadowboxes restlessly, and barks out angry orders and insults. He is observed to be "goin' ape" by cohort Twenty Years (Knox)—an apt description, as his behavior is erratic and his lines often delivered as muffled grunts (in fact, when one turns on the closed captions—a near necessity due to the film's sound problems—many subtitles simply read as "grunt" or "unintelligible sound"). While on the surface this performance may appear to be aimless bluster, subtle pieces of evidence point to Mailer's self-awareness of this acting style, which in turn suggests an embedded criticism of his own behavior. When Mailer speaks his early lines, for example, the camera zooms in on his face, which often displays a sly grin. Moreover, there is more than one scene where Prince is filmed looking in the mirror, but also looking directly at the audience through his reflection, thus drawing attention to his own character as a cinematic construction.

We might also see some of these scenes as winking nods to hyperbolic reflections of Mailer in the character of Prince. As Mailer himself stated, "Since I've been a sort of notorious—if you will—character all these years, it was inevitable that I should make movies."[15] The exaggerated performance he offers in *Wild 90* seems to recursively refer to this "notorious character" that he and the public have shaped together. Mailer was certainly aware of maintaining both a public and a private self, his "real" identity (if, in fact, such a thing can be said to exist) refracted across his various roles. His glimpses in the mirror offer a sense of this self-awareness and multiplicity, forcing the audience to wonder whether they are seeing Prince in the mirror, Mailer in the mirror, or Mailer's public persona in the mirror. A similar effect is achieved in Prince's comments at the end of *Wild 90*. Turning directly to face the camera this time, rather than merely glancing at it surreptitiously through his reflection, Prince says, "I wanna talk to the audience: may I have the camera on me please." He goes on to say that viewers have been watching this courtesy of the CIA, and adds (with another surreptitious grin) that he has been reading Norman Mailer—his favorite author, naturally. All of these comments are references to *being watched*, both within the context of the film and, perhaps, in his own life as the "real" Norman Mailer. In breaking down the cinematic fourth wall here, he has called into question any notion of what is real versus what is performance, a stylistic choice that underscores the film's interrogation of its own representations.

The film's occasionally ridiculous and generally aimless dialogue, however, often disguises this underlying message. For example, the film opens with Prince, Twenty Years, and Cameo (Farbar) engaged in a childish back and forth about whose feet smell worse, and they continue to trade insults about being fat, cheap, lazy, and feminine (on more than one occasion, one accuses another of having "no balls"). Though this dialogue tests the audience's patience, its presence (indeed, its persistence) is key to what Mailer called the film's "comedy of manners," and it enhances the ironies and contradictions of the work.[16] In other words, the dialogue allows the film to be a comic meditation of the characters' behavior as well as a serious evaluation: in its very exaggeration, it mocks the same overblown machismo it performs, exposing the paradoxical fragility of the tough-guy pose. This may have been what Mailer was attempting to explain in his essay "Some Dirt in the Talk," when he said that "bona fide tough guys, invited for nothing, usually laugh their heads off at the film" while "white collar workers and intellectual technicians of the communications industries . . . tend to regard the picture in a vault of silence."[17] That is, the tough guys get it not because they are inherently more masculine than other viewers, but because they understand the joke: they see through the performance straight to the posturing, because the "tough guy" himself is a character. If anything, Mailer makes that macho performance even easier to see in this film than in "real" life, simply because the characters are so obviously presenting an inflated front. As he says, *Wild 90* is funny precisely because it "is filled with nothing so much as these vanities, bluffs, ego-supports, and downright collapses of front."[18]

Moreover, Mailer had complex and specific notions of what masculinity is, and the masculinity performed in *Wild 90* does not reflect these definitions. As he would state repeatedly throughout his career, masculinity is something that must be earned. A man must test his courage, stare down the existential abyss, and fight for his manhood. "Masculinity is not something given to you, something you're born with, but something you gain," Mailer wrote in *Cannibals and Christians.* "And you gain it by winning small battles with honor" (242). *Wild 90* displays no such test of courage, nor do any of the characters appear to win any recognizable, honorable battles. As Mailer himself notes, the characters in his film are "snarling on the bone, not kingpins of the rackets now, but rather back to adolescence, hoods on the corner."[19] They are not men, but boys—or more accurately, men acting like boys. The film observes the way men try valiantly to fit some preexisting notion of masculinity that includes swearing, touting weapons, lobbing insults, and differentiating themselves from the feminine by using all manner of offensive epithets to describe women. Ultimately, we laugh at these characters not because they perform these masculinities poorly, but because their foundational assumption that this is what it means to be masculine is so misguided as to seem comic.

Beyond the Law, also filmed over the course of just a few days in 1967, bears some similarities to *Wild 90*—it too is unscripted and, constructed as a series of interviews between cops and criminals during a night in a police station, also makes reference to the ideas of performance and being watched. Here, each character (the cast again a cadre of Mailer's friends) takes on a specific role: either cop or criminal. The film follows the interrogations of the motley crew of criminalized characters brought into the station, from prostitutes to murderers to thieves. Mailer plays Lieutenant Francis Xavier Pope, a tough Irish cop with a reputation for aggressively questioning his suspects. Though his performance in *Beyond the Law* is still relatively theatrical, it is more restrained than his portrayal of Prince in *Wild 90*; the "criminals" are the true stars.

In Mailer's mind, the cop and the criminal were closely related, each serving as the other's alter ego—an idea he emphasizes not only in *Beyond the Law* but in novels like *An American Dream* and, later, in *Tough Guys Don't Dance.* In fact, Francis Xavier Pope of *Beyond the Law* seems to bear a distinct resemblance to Roberts, the tortured detective in charge of Stephen Rojack's murder case in *An American Dream.* As Sara Jo Cohen has noted, "Mailer's Lieutenant Pope inhabits the body of the cop in order to mock him and to illustrate a psyche more tortured than that of the criminal"—an analysis that could certainly apply to Roberts as well.[20] *Beyond the Law* further blurs the lines between the categories of cop and criminal, examining the nature of guilt, innocence, and corruption. Some of the individuals brought into the station confess to the crimes of which they are accused, in some cases remorsefully and in others unapologetically. Some deny having committed a crime at all. In certain cases viewers are led to believe in the innocence of the accused, while in others we are asked to question it. The police officers themselves inhabit ambiguous territory, sometimes seeming to embody not just tortured psyches but potentially criminal behavior, more than the criminals themselves.

The investigation of these various psyches on film, in an unscripted manner, contributes to the kind of self-reflection that is also a central feature of *Wild 90*. "I'm interested in hearing people confront themselves," Lieutenant Pope says—and that also seems to be Mailer's main focus in the film. Mailer makes significant use of the close-up, zooming in on actors' faces as they offer their confessions. Thus, even as Mailer moves quickly back and forth between the different interviews in the station, never staying too long with one character or narrative (part of the reason this film may be more engrossing than his first), the viewer is still left with the impression of having gleaned some insight into each of these characters.

Maidstone, filmed in 1968 but not released until 1970, follows a collection of actors auditioning for a role in the latest movie project from Norman Kingsley (played by Mailer). Kingsley, in addition to being a renowned director, is also considering a presidential run, and may or may not be the focus of a planned assassination attempt. On one level, the film's plot can be seen as Mailer's reflection on the perils of celebrity (with Kingsley serving as another fictional alter ego for Mailer). However, it is also a reflection on the recent assassinations in America—of JFK in 1963, and of Martin Luther King Jr. and Robert Kennedy in 1968—and the culture of fear and tension that this shocking violence had nurtured.

To lend further authenticity to his storyline, Mailer extended unusual autonomy to his assistant directors and cast, encouraging them to develop theoretical assassination plots and construct scenes without his knowledge; as a result, many observed the atmosphere during filming to be tense and infused with paranoia. Mailer noted that, compared to *Beyond the Law, Maidstone* was "a film of no simple premise and much complexity."[21] That is, while the earlier film offered the limited scenario and confined setting of a cop/criminal interrogation scenario to help structure the improvisation, *Maidstone* was much more unpredictable; this was compounded by Mailer's choice to relinquish much more control as a director, which added to his own sense of tension on set. He would later recognize "his own blunder in giving so much autonomy to [actor Rip] Torn and the other assistant directors."[22]

Maidstone is also the most notorious of Mailer's three experimental films, largely due to the movie's climactic scene. On the last day of filming, after Mailer had sent the majority of his cast home, Rip Torn (who played Kingsley's half-brother in the film) decided to remain in character and attack Mailer, as one final attempt at the "assassination." Mailer was stunned and angry, and their faux fight quickly became real, resulting in both men bloodied: Torn struck Mailer with a hammer and Mailer then bit into Torn's ear. All of this was captured on camera, as were the reactions of Mailer's children and then-wife, Beverly Bentley, who had been visiting Mailer on set. Though Mailer was furious with Torn and vowed to cut the scene, he eventually proffered his belief that "Torn had been right to make his attack. . . . Without it there was not enough" to the film's conclusion.[23] Despite the difficulties and drama surrounding its making, Mailer ultimately expresses his satisfaction with much of the work of *Maidstone.* "It was possible *Maidstone* inhabited that place where the film was supposed to live—that hallway station between the psychological and the real which helped to explain the real," he explained.[24] Mailer expressed a similar notion of the purpose of film in "Some Dirt in the Talk." There, he confessed his belief that the film without a script is more akin to a dream, whereupon the actors can map out the future: that dream, he stated, is "a theatrical revue which dramatizes the dangers of the day—a production in which the world of the day is dissected, exaggerated, put together again in dramatic or even surrealist intensity in order to test the power of the nervous system."[25]

"Making a film is a cross between a circus, a military campaign, a nightmare, an orgy, and a high," Mailer once said.[26] Though this eclectic description highlights precisely why the process of filmmaking was so exhilarating for Mailer, it also highlights why it was exhausting, and the financial toll of his films, coupled with their mixed reviews and lack of commercial success, contributed to Mailer's decision to set aside filmmaking for the time being. After *Maidstone,* he would make only one more film, *Tough Guys Don't Dance,* based on his 1984 novel of the same name. Although he briefly contemplated a long hiatus from writing in order to pursue further directorial efforts, Mailer never completely removed himself from the literary world in which he was such a central figure. In fact, directly after wrapping *Maidstone,* Mailer wrote and published *Miami and the Siege of Chicago*. In this work, he once again makes himself a character in his own observational narrative, referring to himself as "the reporter" as he covers the Republican convention in Miami and the Democratic convention in Chicago. As he moves through the conventions, Mailer as "the reporter" reflects upon himself as much as he does the individuals around him. For example, consider the account of Mailer's first impression of the Republican convention:

"The reporter had moved through the convention quietly, as anonymously as possible, wan, depressed, troubled. Something profoundly unclassifiable was going on among the Republicans and he did not know if it was conceivably good or a concealment of something bad—which was the first time a major social phenomenon like a convention had confused him so" (14).

Here, Mailer not only describes the ambiance surrounding the convention, but reflects on his own involvement and understanding of it as well, worrying about his ability to responsibly and accurately report the conventions he is covering. He admits, for instance, that he felt confident covering the 1960 and 1964 conventions, but this "was a different affair—one could not tell if nothing much was going on, or to the contrary, nothing much was going on near the surface but everything was shifting down below" (14–15). To him, Nixon is "the most interesting figure at the convention" (50), which Mailer finds "too peaceful by far" (66), and he feels a kind of pitied respect for the "new," more subdued Nixon, anticipating him as the clear winner over the more naive opponent Nelson "Rocky" Rockefeller.[27]

Despite this somewhat blasé overview of the politics of the Republican convention, Mailer pans out to brilliantly capture some of the absurdity of the environment surrounding the candidates themselves. For example, he casually throws in references to the "Nixon girls" doing high kicks like Rockettes, their antics seemingly aimed at adding a bit of flair to an otherwise bland convention. He depicts the jarring disparity of the Poor People's Campaign demonstrating outside of a convention that is populated largely by wealthy conservatives. The attendees themselves are essentially depicted as a series of grotesques: "Most of them were ill-proportioned in some part of their physique. . . . The dowager's hump was common, and many a man had a flaccid paunch, but the collective tension was rather in the shoulders, in the girdling of the shoulders against anticipated lashings on the back" (35).

This mildly comic affair of the Republic convention stands in stark contrast to his observations of the chaos surrounding the Democratic convention in Chicago. The protests and riots that erupted outside of the convention lend a much more serious tension to the event, creating an undercurrent of simmering anxiety that runs through Mailer's narrative. Though Mailer does cover the convention itself, referencing the platforms and appeals (or lack thereof) of candidates Hubert Humphrey and Eugene McCarthy, he quickly acknowledges that an account of the convention is not an accurate description of "the event." The "event" was the "five-day battle in the streets and parks of Chicago between some of the minions of the high established, and some of the nihilistic of the young," the former being the Chicago police and political authorities (including Mayor Daley), and the latter being the Students for a Democratic

Society (SDS), the Youth International Party (Yippies), and the National Mobilization Committee (the Mobe), who were staging legal anti–Vietnam War demonstrations near the convention center (131). At first, demonstrations were relatively peaceful; however, protesters and police soon clashed in Grant Park and Lincoln Park, with police using tear gas to evacuate demonstrators. When police officers attacked a demonstrator who had been attempting to take down an American flag at a Grant Park rally, chaos ensued. Thousands of people poured onto Michigan Avenue to march in protest, but police halted the march at Balbo Avenue, holding demonstrators for nearly half an hour before inexplicably launching a barrage of tear gas, Mace, and physical violence on the crowd.

Mailer describes the brimming violence amid the rioters in the streets poetically, drawing attention to his own detachment from the chaos below. He explains the way the police "attacked like a scythe through grass" and cut through the crowd "like a razor cutting a channel through a head of hair" (169). As he watches through a window in the relative safety of the Hyatt overlooking Michigan Avenue, Mailer observes that, "seen from the nineteenth floor, it was like a wind blowing dust, or the edge of waves riding foam on the shore," and notes that "there was something of the detachment of studying a storm at evening through a glass, the light was a lovely gray-blue, the police had uniforms of sky blue, even the ferocity had an abstract elemental play of forces of nature at battle with other forces" (169). In this moment, it is as though the tumult below slows down for Mailer and becomes almost surreal, and he feels acutely apart from the cause taken up by the protesters.

In fact, in contrast to his involvement in the political protest during the march on the Pentagon, Mailer felt detached from the demonstrations throughout the duration of the convention. In his mind, "The justifications of the March on the Pentagon" were not present in Chicago, even though the crowds gathering in Lincoln Park and Grant Park were also protesting the war in Vietnam. Though he does visit Lincoln Park, where the Yippie demonstrators are protesting the war, and finds fellow literary heavyweights Allen Ginsberg, Jean Genet, and William Burroughs are also there (Genet and Burroughs were covering the event for *Esquire*), Mailer's relative ambivalence about the protest prompts him to leave. As he explains, "The reporter was a literary man—symbol had the power to push him into actions more heroic than himself. The fact that he had been marching to demonstrate against a building which was the living symbol of everything he most despised—the military-industrial complex of the land—had worked to fortify his steps. . . . But in Chicago, there was no symbol for him" (144). Hence his decision to remain distant from the fray on Michigan Avenue (which he refers to as a "massacre"). He does sense the "air of outrage, hysteria, panic, fury, madness, gallows humor, and gloom" hanging over the nominations, and does eventually make his way across Michigan Avenue after the crowds have thinned. Mailer's journalistic endeavor ends this time not with an arrest, but with a semi-friendly tousle with a police officer, then a night of drinking at the Playboy mansion (176).

Mailer makes several attempts to rationalize his decision to remain apart from the crowds, trying to make sense of it, though he also criticizes himself for these rationalizations. His excuse—that one of his friends, "a professional boxer . . . would probably be unable to keep himself from taking out six or eight men" if violence were to erupt—seems tepid for Mailer, and he himself seems to know this: "He was either being sensible, militarily sensible, revolutionary in the hard way of facing into twenty years of a future like this . . . or he was yellow" (148). In fact, Mailer focuses quite a bit on his fear, noting that in Chicago it "had grown dimensions" and "structure" (186). "One simply could not accept the dangerous alternative every time; he would never do any other work," he says (186). As he muses: "He liked his life. He wanted it to go on, which meant that he wanted America to go on—not as it was going, not Vietnam—but what price was he really willing to pay? . . . To be forty-five years old, and have lost a sense of where his loyalties belonged—to the revolution or to the stability of the country (at some painful personal price it could be suggested) was to bring upon himself the anguish of the European intellectual in the Thirties" (188).

This is a significant moment for Mailer, the man who in works such as "The White Negro" and *An American Dream* embraced danger and violence as an outlet for individual strength, creativity, and freedom. Yet when confronted with its actual rather than ideological form, Mailer begins to question his own avid pronouncements more strongly. It is also significant that he does so publicly, in his writing, not shying away from the uncertainties that plague him out of any fear of embarrassment or accusations of waffling. Later, in *The Big Empty,* Mailer further reflects on the ambivalence that characterized many individual reactions to these demonstrations. As he writes, "liberals did react against the open, ugly and unforgettable spectacle of the police smashing into the front ranks of the marchers, but even more voters felt that anarchy was loose in the street, so they blamed the marchers for aggravating the cops . . . in America, the reluctance to cause disturbance is always sitting there in opposition to the other big American desire—which is to express oneself, to be free and free-spoken" (31).

Despite Mailer's relatively subdued involvement in the conventions in Miami and Chicago (so far as one can call a trip that ends with drinking at the Playboy mansion "subdued"), he nevertheless continued to involve himself enthusiastically and publicly in the ongoing political and cultural conversation in America, contributing his incisive commentary on a number of different topics. One of the most significant of these was the moon landing in 1969, which Mailer chronicled in his 1970 publication, *Of a Fire on the Moon*. In this work, Mailer again refers to himself in the third person, naming himself "Aquarius," not only because this is his astrological sign, but because the mythical figure of Aquarius, the "water bearer," had "traversed the earth and breathed the air: three elements were his medium, solid, liquid, and gas. That was akin to the rocket" (6).

While the nation celebrates Apollo 11's successful landing on the moon, Mailer approaches the historical and scientific breakthrough with characteristic skepticism. He confesses that he "did not know how he felt" because "for all he knew, Apollo-Saturn was still a child of the Devil. . . . the notion that man voyaged out to fulfill the desire of God was either the heart of the vision, or anathema to that true angel in Heaven they would violate by the fires of their ascent" (103). In other words, in his vision of good and evil waging a constant war, Mailer is not sure which side space travel favors. In a different sense, Mailer fears humanity is embodying the myth of Icarus, overreaching its bounds—though in this case, flying too close to the moon.

Another cause for Mailer's hesitance to wholeheartedly embrace the moon mission lies in criticisms of technology—something of which he had long been critical, as he felt technology to be the enemy of critical thinking, growth, and magic. As Barry Leeds aptly summarizes, "The situation presented Mailer in *Of a Fire on the Moon* is not a happy one for him. He is forced to confront the possibility that the technology oriented people of the establishment may, finally, have won the moon because in their dogged, unimaginative way they have earned the right to, while artists, intellectuals, and dropouts have submerged themselves in a lifestyle which has a sterility of its own."[28] Indeed, as Mailer points out after transcribing one of the many conversations between the astronauts and base control in Houston, "Beautiful data was clear and thorough data. An engineer's idea of beauty was system perfection. Beauty was obviously the absence of magic" (311). In a commentary that eerily predicts some of the very criticisms that have become magnified since the advent of the Internet, Mailer fears that the "digital computer was not a machine which would force men to think in new ways about the environment, it was rather an electronic mode of calculating which might yet change the nature of thought itself (352). It is "plastic brainpower" that might accelerate "the rush to extermination" (357).

Mailer's skepticism does not cloud his awe at the scientific accomplishments of NASA, nor his appreciation of the feats of engineering that contributed to the Apollo 11 mission. Indeed, much of *Of a Fire on the Moon* is comprised of Mailer's detailed description of the science behind the moon landing. While much of the world focused its attention on astronauts Neil Armstrong, Buzz Aldrin, and Michael Collins, Mailer devotes a significant amount of space to the work going on behind the scenes. Nevertheless, as he approaches the deadline for his manuscript covering the event, he finds himself unsettled and unsatisfied, confessing that this was a "sex-stripped mystery of machines which might have a mind, and mysterious men who managed to live like machines" (467). He is also left wondering: "Was the voyage of Apollo 11 the noblest expression of a technological age, or the best evidence of its utter insanity?" (382). Even after the success of the mission, this question is left unanswered; the moon landing is, for Mailer, a symbol of the unknown future, and of a shift in the times, toward a culture that rejects magic in favor of technology, and perhaps one that rejects creativity in favor of "system perfection." Ultimately, the moon landing reflects back to him a world "half convinced of the future death of our species yet half aroused by the apocalyptic notion that an exceptional future still lay before us. So it was a century which moved with the most magnificent display of power into directions it could not comprehend" (48).

During this time, as part of his ongoing commentary on American cultural shifts and events, Mailer also began to engage more often with the second-wave feminist movement—often in ways that stirred up a significant amount of controversy. Mailer's media appearances at this time (when he was still at the height of his celebrity) would frequently land him in hot water, largely as a result of his comments on women's liberation. Perhaps his most famous engagement with this topic, however, is the 1971 Town Hall panel, featuring central figures of the second-wave feminist movement, including Germaine Greer, National Organization of Women president Jacqueline Ceballos, journalist Jill Johnston, and literary critic Diana Trilling, a longtime friend of Mailer's. During the panel (later dubbed "Town Bloody Hall" by Greer), Mailer—the sole male panelist—becomes the target of the audience's ire, a representative of the patriarchal society against which they were fighting. Though visibly frustrated with the ways that some of the speeches at the event would veer away from serious discussion of gender and women's rights, Mailer courts argument, fueling the fiery debate. In other words, despite being under fire, Mailer (who loved an argument) also appears to be enjoying himself.

The audience and panelists at Town Bloody Hall were, in large part, taking Mailer to task for his recent remarks about gender and women's rights in his 1971 book, *The Prisoner of Sex*. However, Mailer's opinions on this matter were not necessarily new, nor were his controversial remarks, which have since become oft-cited sound bites. For instance, nearly a decade earlier, in an interview with Paul Krassner, Mailer had made comments reducing women to stereotypes, asserting that "the prime responsibility of a woman probably is to be on earth long enough to find the best mate possible for herself, and conceive children who will improve the species." Thus, he continues, "if they start looking for pills which prevent conception, then what they're doing . . . is acting like the sort of people who take out a new automobile and put sand in the crank case in order to see if the sound that the motor gives off is a new sound."[29] This kind of comment, which neglects to take into account the significant role birth control played (and still plays) in gender equality, not to mention the ability of women to take control of their own reproductive health, rankled women across the nation, and contributed to Mailer's reputation as one of the foremost antagonists of second-wave feminism. Remarks like these followed Mailer around for much of his life, and were a contributing factor to his coming under fire at the Town Hall forum.

Even Mailer himself seemed to be aware of the hole he had dug himself into during his interview with Krassner. There, for example, Krassner asks whether the decision to have the protagonist of Mailer's short story "The Time of Her Time" call his penis the "avenger" doesn't imply "a certain hostility to women." Mailer replies simply, "Of course it does. Is that news?" His frustrated reply, tinged with sarcasm, suggests that he is well aware of the controversy stirred up by the tale, and perhaps is not entirely in agreement with the accusation; furthermore, he is quick to discourage anyone from merging his identity with that of his protagonist. He also goes on to say: "I'm hostile to men, I'm hostile to women, I'm hostile to cats, to poor cockroaches, I'm afraid of horses. You know" (132). Still, in the same breath, he muses, "I would guess that most men who understand women at all feel hostility toward them. At their worst, women are low sloppy beasts" (131). Whether or not such statements were tongue-in-cheek—and they may have been intended as such—they did not do him any favors with the feminist movement of the time. Yet for better or worse, these remarks sparked debate, and it is likely that this is precisely what he was seeking. While Mailer may not have been able to predict the level of backlash he would receive from his comments, he embraced controversy and bombast and argument—and his engagement with the feminist movement provided these in spades.

This engagement is most evident in *The Prisoner of Sex*, Mailer's careful meditation on gender. Mailer wrote the book after spending a summer in Maine alone with his six children, essentially running house and home for several weeks. The domestic duties he took on there helped to facilitate his ongoing consideration of the prescribed gender roles in American society, and the book itself—though problematic in a number of ways—is also a testament to Mailer's investment in dialogue and intellectual discussion. His musings, theories, literary exegeses, and self-reflections demonstrate that he does not want to be an obstacle or antagonist to women's liberation, nor is he "anti-feminist"; however, his treatise does also exhibit a number of mystifying comments about women that threaten to unravel his otherwise thoughtful exposition.

From the beginning of the book, Mailer attempts to understand why his reputation, as he puts it, "had not only been ambushed but was apparently being chewed half to death by a squadron of enraged Amazons, an honor guard of revolutionary (if we would have them) vaginas" (15). Here Mailer's tone is halfway between seriousness and mockery—a tone that crops up several times throughout the work and makes many of his statements somewhat difficult to analyze. Some of this may be chalked up to the fact that many of his comments might simply be aimed to stir up more controversy, and invite argument. As Mailer himself states, "To be the center of any situation was . . . the real marrow of his bone—better to expire as a devil in the fire than an angel in the wings" (17). Reflecting on his own remark that "women should be kept in cages" (a line delivered on a 1970 television program with Orson Welles), he says that he "was pleased with himself, pleased that he might be the last of the public entertainers to cut such an outsized hunk of remark in the teeth of growing piety over treatment of women" (24). Orson Welles interpreted this comment as misogynistic, which is precisely what Mailer expected—he was looking for an argument, he wanted to sustain the dialogue—but he also admits, contrary to serious intentions, that "the impulse to clown was inevitable" (25). These competing impulses are evident throughout *The Prisoner of Sex,* wherein Mailer continues to waffle between compassion for the plight of women and ultimate adherence to notions of masculinity and femininity that contribute to gendered discrimination in America.

Early on in *Prisoner,* in a section titled "The Acolyte," Mailer is candid about how much he does not yet know about women. For example, he exhibits surprise regarding the writings of women like Germaine Greer, who were able to write, as he saw it, like men. Of Greer's writing, he says, "A wind in this prose whistled up the kilts of male conceit. The base of male conceit was that men could live with truths too unsentimental for women to support; now women were writing about men and about themselves as Henry Miller had once written about women" (34). This leads Mailer to admit that "he had much to learn on many a familiar topic" (34), a comment that shows promise—suggesting he might, after further consideration, dispel the notion that women are simply writing "like men" and acknowledge that they are instead writing like themselves, as they finally can after years of being told they must write in the voice of some misguided, socially constructed notion of "the feminine."

Moreover, as he attempts to make sense of the women's lib movement of the 1960s and 1970s, Mailer carefully considers the language of published feminists like Greer (whom he cautiously admires) and Kate Millett (whose *Sexual Politics* he sharply criticizes). One of the major obstacles to his truly understanding the goals of the movement, however, is his investment in notions of gender that assign men and women to prescriptive roles, largely as a result of biological differences. Though he acknowledges, "The womb was a damnable disadvantage in the struggle with men, a cranky fouled-up bag of horrors for any woman who would stand equal to men on modern jobs," he claims that it allows women to be "a step, or a stage, or a move or a leap nearer the creation of existence," and "they were—given man's powerful sense of the present—his indispensable and only connection to the future" (47). For this reason, Mailer harbors an idea of woman as inherently "mystical." While Mailer intends to flatter and demonstrate respect for woman's ability to create, he instead reifies the notion that woman is (as Simone de Beauvoir had lamented in *The Second Sex*) primarily defined as a womb. Mailer says that what a woman sees as the "burden of her womb" is "a privileged element of nature, closer to the mysteries than men" (48). And perhaps many women might have seen it as such. Yet this is not the claim of women's lib, to whom Mailer is purportedly responding, and in aiming to convince the reader that the womb is a gift rather than a curse, he is missing the message and the hurdle that women are trying to overcome.

Due to his ideas of the mysticism and power attached to the womb, Mailer is terrified of technology encroaching on procreation—artificial insemination and birth control repulse him. Contraception, he believes, makes sex into a "transaction—when no hint remains of the awe that a life in these circumstances can be conceived" (124). In a particularly bizarre theoretical interlude, he suggests that "a woman can even search the most isolated ducts of her body for every quality she wishes to slip or to fling into the future" just as "an unhealthy woman might dispose of a quintessential malaise or chasm or rot through a pregnancy she knows will miscarry or go to abort" (139). He suggests that in the past women could "sacrifice any of their ova if the man does not suit the preciosities of their theme" and that "planned parenthood originated in the psyche of many a lady long before contraceptives" (143). Such a mystifying, unfounded idea would startle even—or perhaps especially—the twenty-first-century reader.

However, Mailer repeatedly circles back to a more serious, rational attempt to understand the gendered inequality in America at the time, offering glimmers of promising insights. He knew, for instance, that "he could not begin to evaluate his relocated view of the ladies until he had reconnoitered his comprehension of men" (53). He does acknowledge the "line of thought which looks to prove that differences between men and women have been exaggerated," and are cultural constructions (94); however, this is a line of thought that Mailer is hesitant to accept. As he says, "His aversion remained to the liberal supposition it was good that men and women become more and more alike; that gave him a species of aesthetic nausea" (98). Throughout the work, Mailer continually refers to his aversion to women seeking the right to "be masculine," which is not necessarily what second-wave feminism asked—women wanted to be women, but they wanted to expand the definition of what women could be, without being accused of trying to be men. In fighting to be treated more "like men" at the time, feminists were asking for equal opportunities and an equally weighted voice. Thus, by insisting that women were not so different from men, they hoped to achieve more equal treatment in the public sphere.

Still, Mailer cannot see or articulate the deeper need for their rhetorical tactic—he is too afraid that similarity will disrupt the social and sexual "balance" achieved by masculinity and femininity (116). "Cultural conditioning to be masculine or feminine may not be the arbitrary exercise of a patriarchal society so much as derive from some instinct or impulse of nature," he insists, arguing that men and women were "inheritors of a male and female personage in their individual psyche" (121). This nature-versus-nurture argument still persists today, even though in all likelihood experiences of gender identity are derived not from one or the other of these options, but both. The difference is that today, after much of the work achieved by feminism (though certainly there is still a ways to go in terms of achieving equality in the political and corporate spheres), women can identify as feminine or masculine or neither or both and still have an opportunity to achieve a position of power. At the time Mailer was writing *The Prisoner of Sex,* it was much more difficult for women to do so—so it was necessary to use a more extreme vocabulary, to deny traditional femininity, and to encourage acceptance of similarities between men and women, in order to be taken seriously.

And thus, when Mailer balked at such suggestions, he may have unwittingly been contributing to an ongoing problem. After all, Mailer himself expressed no desire to keep women out of the workplace. Mailer says he "is not nostalgic" for the "feminine mystique," and "all his enthusiasm for the mystery of the womb is not to squeeze women back into that old insane shoe" (128), a comment which is further supported by remarks he made in *The Armies of the Night,* where he said that the houses of liberals "look one like the other, for the wives gave up herculean careers as doctors, analysts, sociologists, anthropologists, labor relations experts—great servants of the social program were lost when the women got married and relinquished all for hubber and kids" (25). By being so hesitant to accept the shifts in perception and language being requested by women's lib, however, his writing threatens to come across as condescending and conservative rather than supportive.

And in the end, he still "felt something like agreement with a balance which would offer men vision and women 'the power of the soul'" (129). His ultimate conclusion is that he would not marry a woman who wanted to divide housework fifty-fifty. "If he were obliged to have a roommate, he would pick a man," he says. "The question had been answered. He could love a women and she might even sprain her back before a hundred sinks of dishes in a month, but he would not be happy to help her if his work should suffer, no, not unless her work was as valuable as his own" (165). Such a conclusion created an impasse between Mailer and those supporting the second-wave feminist movement, and comments like these certainly contributed to the antagonism and tension that defined the panel at Town Bloody Hall just a few months after the book's publication. There, Mailer came as ready for a heated debate as always, aware that he would be a target—and relishing it. As he says in *Prisoner,* "He was equal to one of those prodigies of paradoxical health who thrive on operation after operation—his literary vitality seemed to derive from being exposed" (23).

CHAPTER 5

Exploring American Mysteries

Mailer's Interpretive Biographies

In addition to his involvement in and commentary on American politics, Mailer took a keen interest in the lives of a number of controversial and elusive American figures throughout the course of his career. In the 1970s, Mailer published several in-depth pieces on such individuals, offering unique, interrogative profiles of Gary Gilmore, Marilyn Monroe, and Muhammad Ali.[1] Of these profiles, *The Executioner's Song,* the nonfictional account of the events leading up to and surrounding Gilmore's conviction and execution, has been one of Mailer's most widely praised works, garnering a Pulitzer Prize in 1980. As a blend of journalism and creative nonfiction, the book exemplifies Mailer's deftness at hybridizing genres, while also revealing his ongoing concerns with themes of existentialism, violence, and redemption. In *The Fight* (1975), an account of the Muhammad Ali–George Foreman fight in Kinshasa, Mailer similarly blurs generic lines, once again making himself a character in his account of the famous "Rumble in the Jungle." Additionally, in his 1973 biography of Marilyn Monroe, Mailer searches for the "real" Marilyn behind the public facade, in much the same way he seeks to uncover grains of truth and authenticity amid the highly publicized lives of Gilmore, Ali, and Foreman. Although Mailer turned his attention to some lengthier fictional works through the 1980s, in the late 1990s he returned to biography, this time examining the lives of Lee Harvey Oswald and Pablo Picasso—two very different figures whose experiences nevertheless seem to fit equally well into Mailer's literary purview.

None of these narratives can be called traditional biographies. Mailer himself has emphasized the interpretive nature of these works, consciously setting them apart from purely "fact-based" life writing. As Michael Glenday has noted, the decision to offer his own personal reflection and speculation on the lives of these famous (and infamous) figures might have polarizing effects on readers, who will either "accept, even relish the prospect of encountering not just the memoir, but also the vitality of interaction between Mailer's imagination and his subject," or they will dismiss such narratives "on grounds of illegitimacy" and "will refuse him admission into the academy of biographers."[2] Yet to deem these works "illegitimate" would be misleading, for Mailer does not simply fabricate storylines for any of his subjects. While he does speculate and hypothesize, he also forces us to question what are often mistakenly framed as the irrefutable facts of these celebrity lives. Human life, Mailer suggests in these works, is not so easily summarized, and the "facts" themselves are often disingenuous or in some cases blatantly false. For example, he observes in *Marilyn* that one set of facts about Monroe's life always seemed to invite a set of opposing facts about her, thus leaving us with more questions than answers. The appeal of his interpretive style, then, is that "he is free to occupy the ground of a psychohistory that leaves room for both romantic and magical explanations of human behavior."[3] These explanations are neither infallible nor always verifiable, but in many cases they reflect the nuanced, complex messiness of individual life.

In 1973, Norman Mailer published *Marilyn,* a biographical profile meant to be a 20,000-word piece, but which Mailer expanded to over 100,000 words after becoming deeply fascinated with Monroe during the writing process.[4] At the center of the work is an obsession with the mystery surrounding Marilyn, from the strange coincidences that Mailer says "spring underfoot like toadstools" throughout the duration of her life to the constant string of contradictions that define her personality (50). In fact, Marilyn would remain such a fixture in Mailer's mind that he would also compose a fictional account of her life, 1980's *Of Women and Their Elegance* (in which he adopts Marilyn's first-person perspective, as a sort of imaginary autobiography). He would then turn this into a play, *Strawhead,* which was performed at the Actors Studio in 1986. Part of Mailer's fascination with Monroe likely arises from the various ways in which aspects of his life so closely resemble those of his subject. Like Marilyn, Mailer struggled with a controversial public image that threatened to overshadow his craft and at times led to misunderstandings and reductive assumptions about his personal character. It was, in fact, an awareness of this potential connection that led producer Larry Schiller to handpick Mailer to pen the original profile of Marilyn, his rationale being that, "if you could get a writer who has been run over by a lot of trucks, like Marilyn was, and found a way to survive each time, like Marilyn did, it might reveal the key to this deeply mysterious woman."[5]

As Mailer himself notes in his biography, the problem was not just that the "real" Marilyn became overshadowed by the public's perception of her, but that, perhaps, there never was a real Marilyn to begin with. Even Marilyn seemed to acknowledge this, noting in what is now one of her most oft-cited quotes that she "belonged to the public and to the world" and "had never belonged to anything or anyone else." The difficulty in chasing the "real" Marilyn, as Mailer writes, is that "the question of her sincerity is almost insurmountable" (83).[6] In an attempt to move away from a reliance on hearsay, Mailer opted not to create a purely factual biography but instead chose to write what he called a "novel in the form of a biography," blending both fact and "factoid" (a term Mailer himself coined in this work) with fiction and speculation. His idea was that such an approach might "possibly be more accurate than a fiction" as it provides more space to truly examine "the interior of many a closed and silent life" (13).

Mailer's feelings toward Marilyn throughout the book are fraught, and at times ambivalent. Often, she is "gorgeous, forgiving, humorous, compliant and tender" (1). She is also an "angel of cinema" (3) and a "presence" (4) onscreen: Mailer praises Marilyn's performance in nearly every one of her movies, noting that she stands out as the sole redeeming factor in even the most abysmal films. Mailer's view of Marilyn is not myopic, however, and he does not mince words when it comes to imparting the details of her less appealing qualities. He draws attention, for example, to the many stories Marilyn told about her own life that seem sure to be either blatant lies at worst or stretched truths at best. Moreover, where she is "a female spurt of wit and sensitive energy," he says she can also "hang like a sloth for days in a muddy-mooded coma"; she can be both "a fountain of charm" and "a dreary bore," "a lover of life" and "a cowardly hyena of death" (5).

Still, the deeper one delves into Mailer's text, the more apparent it becomes that he loves Marilyn precisely because her life is messy and filled with these contradictions. In a sentence oddly reminiscent of his description of the hipster in "The White Negro," Mailer reminds us that "exceptional people [. . .] had a way of living with opposites in themselves that could only be called schizophrenic" (10). Marilyn, in his mind, was one of those people, unable to be completely understood because her opposites seem always to be at war with one another. For better or worse, the public often tried to confine Marilyn to a single role: as the sexpot, the naïf, the ditzy blonde, and at times the home-wrecker, but to Mailer she is all of these and more. That embodiment of contradiction and multiplicity of character is what intrigues him, for it makes her "a woman with two personalities, each as complex and inconsistent as an individual," and "both are true, and always both, she is the whole and double soul of every human alive" (131–32). This complexity may have contributed to the alluring enigma that came to define Marilyn's persona, but also fashioned her into a conundrum that even she herself could not wholly decipher. That is, the difficulty in unraveling the ambiguities and obscurities that mark Marilyn's personality seems to be that she herself was never quite sure who she was. Early in his profile, Mailer expresses a hope that his literary treatment of Marilyn might better interrogate her interior life, for as he suggests, "It is possible that there is no instrument more ready to capture the elusive quality of her nature than a novel" (13). In the end, Mailer's exploration of her contradictions does effectively represent this elusiveness—but much of Marilyn's mystery defies capture.

Nevertheless, the insights Mailer does offer into Marilyn's character are likely a result of his own engagement with the perils of celebrity. Marilyn's downfall, he suggests, lay in her act of giving too much of herself to the public. Of her early professional successes, Mailer says that "the likelihood and the tragedy is that these are the years when she is giving more of herself than she will get back, and for too little, so that later when she is in love she will be able to offer less and must demand more—at the least we know that she cultivates her sexual sweetmeats in the sexlands of swamp and plague" (107). Still, as Mailer also emphasizes, Marilyn's giving over of herself is also driven, somewhat paradoxically, by her narcissism. "We are all steeped in the notion that lonely withdrawn people have a life of large inner fantasy. What may be ignored is the tendency to become locked in a lifelong rapture with one's fantasy, to become a narcissist" (47). Because much of Marilyn's life, particularly her early childhood, was characterized by loneliness, Mailer theorizes that she retreated into that imaginative part of her psyche as a kind of coping mechanism, thus creating a "fragmented identity" that may have contributed to her depression. Fittingly, then, Mailer's last chapter—a lament over the sadness of her final days—is titled "Lonely Lady," and one of his final assessments is simply that she "leaves in mystery" (302).

Mailer continues to chase mysteries—this time, the magic of boxing—in *The Fight* (1975). This was by no means Mailer's first foray into boxing journalism. He had also covered the famous Patterson-Liston fight in 1962 in a piece for *Esquire* called "Ten Thousand Words a Minute," penned "An Appreciation of Cassius Clay" in 1967 for *Partisan Review,* covered the 1971 Ali-Frazier fight in "King of the Hill" for *Life,* and in 1993 wrote on his own experience boxing at the Gramercy Gym in "The Best Move Lies Close to the Worst," also published in *Esquire.*

In all of these pieces, Mailer expounds on the existential and moral aspects of boxing. For example, after Ali was defeated by Frazier in the 1971 fight, Mailer writes, "Ali had shown America what we all had hoped was secretly true. He was a man. He could bear moral and physical torture and he could stand. And if he could beat Frazier in the rematch we would have at last a national hero who was hero of the world as well."[7] This association between boxing, moral courage, and existential leadership also appears in novels like *The Deer Park, An American Dream,* and *Tough Guys Don't Dance,* in which boxing is a part the protagonists' respective histories and is intricately connected to their notions of masculine courage. As Barry Leeds has noted, for these men, boxing is "applicable to their existential quests for self."[8] Thus, for Mailer, a study of boxing is also a study of masculine selfhood.

Reflecting on the significant presence of boxing in Mailer's canon, Ronald Fried has noted that "boxing was important to Mailer because, during his lifetime, boxing was important to America," for it "occupied a more central place in the national psyche: it raised racial and political issues thanks to such irresistibly complex figures as Muhammad Ali, Joe Frazier, Floyd Patterson, and Sonny Liston."[9] In *The Fight,* Mailer's attempt to find the source of this irresistible complexity is evident in his multidimensional approach to boxing. The piece is part investigative reporting, part detached observation, and part personal narrative, an example of Mailer's tendency to move in and out of styles in order to find the voice that allows him to best explore his subject. Throughout the narrative, he takes on the role of an investigator as he probes the mystery and superstition that drives boxing culture, while also offering a clear journalistic portrait of Ali's preparation of the fight in the role of a more detached reporter.

He also reflects on his own physical and mental strength in the presence of Ali in particular, thus effectively adding an element of autobiography to this interpretive biography. To enhance this effect, Mailer once again makes himself a character in his own reportage, this time acknowledging such a narrative tactic to be a "vice" but a necessary one, for in his coverage of the event he became a part of it and thus had "his own small effect on events" (31). While this would, he knows, inevitably lead some critics to address his "ego trips and the unattractive dimensions of his narcissism," he is relatively unfazed (31). His goal is not to turn the attention solely on himself, but to personalize the narrative in order to make it more intimate. As he says, "He had already had a love affair with himself, and it used up a good deal of love. He was no longer so pleased with his presence" (31). Notably, *The Fight* is also the last in a series of books in which Mailer writes about himself in the third person, making himself a central figure, thus proving that in fact his "love affair with himself" may indeed have been waning.

Mailer does, in fact, demonstrate a distinct humility in *The Fight* as he measures himself against Ali and Foreman. His aim is not necessarily to prove himself physically against the fighters; even Mailer realizes such a goal is unrealistic, recounting in detail his struggle to keep up with Ali during a brief training run. Rather, he aims to demonstrate that there is some other kind of kinship between himself and Ali, and that the art of boxing is not so dissimilar from the art of writing—despite Ali's claim to the press that "you who write about boxing are ignorant of what you describe" (65). After all, as Joyce Carol Oates later wrote in *On Boxing,* "Each boxing match is a story—a unique and highly condensed drama without words" where boxers are "characters in the literary sense of the word. *Extravagant fictions without a structure to contain them.*"[10]

As Oates also argues, "Mailer's strength lies in his recognition that the boxers are *other*—though he does not say so. . . . it seems clear to the reader at least that Mailer cannot establish a connection to the boxers," even if he "tries heroically."[11] While Mailer may have never been able to truly grasp the psyche of boxers like Ali and Foreman, he remained dedicated to rendering their characters, and to finding the language that could in some way evoke their "extravagant fictions." In his portrait of Foreman, he expresses admiration of the latter's skill and strength, noting that "the violence capable of being generated in a champion like Foreman is staggering to contemplate" and that Foreman was "a physical genius who employed the methods of catatonia (silence, concentration and immobility)" (47). He also notes that Ali "was a genius in wholly separate ways" (47). Ali "was ready for oncoming chaos, ready for the volcanic disruptions that would boil through the world in these approaching years of pollution, malfunction, and economic disaster"; he was "living with a vision of himself as a world leader" (79). As a result of these fundamental differences of psyche and spirit, Mailer predicts that "the fight would then be a religious war" (47).

In addition to probing the boxer's psyches and attempting to articulate their appeal and, in some cases, their almost otherworldly essence, Mailer also explores the mystical quality of boxing in general, which in part made the sport both an engrossing and a terrifying experience for the spectator. Years earlier, in "Ten Thousand Words a Minute," Mailer had expounded on the superstition and magic that propels boxing. Writing about a party prior to that earlier fight between Patterson and Liston, he says that a "mood of expectation, of omen and portent," preoccupied everyone. It seemed as though "all of one's small actions became significant," to the extent that even his choice of taxi cabs to the event seems plagued by this ominous, supernatural bent: "One had the psychology of a ghost choosing the hearse he would ride to a funeral."[12] Likewise, in *The Fight,* Mailer describes boxing as a somewhat preternatural sport, drawing from the Bantu philosophy of *n'golo,* a Congolese word for one's vital force (of "ego, status, strength or libido") to explain the source of its power (75). In Mailer's description, the smallest shift in chance or karma or human action can strengthen or deprive one of n'golo. At one point, for instance, Ali and his manager Bundini fight over which robe Ali will wear into the ring, a spat that threatens to ruin the mood prior to the fight. As Mailer writes, Bundini's expression seemed to say, "*don't mess with the wisdom of your man. I bought a robe which matches my jacket. Your strength and my strength are linked. Weaken me, and you weaken yourself. Wear the colors I have chosen*" (167). Here, an otherwise arbitrary garment takes on new significance with the potential to diminish Ali's "vital force," a significance seemingly derived from the tenuous but powerful magic that surrounds his sport.

Mailer's fixation on circling parapets also plays a role in his representation of boxing and superstition, and it further offers him a way to make himself a key player in the events of the fight. After attending a party prior to the match, Mailer decides to scale the balcony outside of his hotel room, climbing "into a squall of magical forces" (123) because "he knew that Muhammad's chances would be greater if he did than if he didn't" (124). Though he later regretted what he describes as an act of risky "vanity," at the time he "was caught in a current which had nothing to do with him" (123). He recalls attempting a similar feat before the Ali-Liston fight, after which Ali tore a groin muscle and that fight was also postponed—events that he feels are also distinctly connected. "How could you ever know with clarity whether the walk on the roof had been connected or absolutely unconnected to Ali's rupture?" he asks. "A small obsession for a magician" (124).

For Mailer, boxing was not only influenced by magic and spirituality, it was also deeply informed by race—or at least, Mailer's perceptions of blackness. As he writes, "Heavyweight boxing was almost all black, black as Bantu. So boxing had become another key to revelations of Black, one more key to black emotion, black psychology, black love" (43). For example, many of Mailer's descriptions of Foreman and Ali are racialized. Mailer claims that Foreman is more intimidating because he seems "more Black" to Mailer—and thus he was "in communion with a muse . . . the muse of violence in all her complexity" (49). Mailer made similar comments about what he perceived to be racial advantages and disadvantages in "Ten Thousand Words a Minute." There, he writes that Sonny Liston had "lived in violence, had grown in violence" (241); he was also involved with the mob, and had been to prison, and as a result,

"Liston was voodoo, Liston was magic, Liston was the pet of the witch doctor; Liston knew that when the gods gathered to watch an event, you kept your mind open to the devils who might work for you" (242). By contrast, what weakens Floyd Patterson in Mailer's view, even though Patterson was supposed to be the "everyman" and the "the hero of all those unsung romantics" (241), is that "the Establishment had made him Negroid white. His skin was black, his psychology was turned white" (260).

Additionally, Mailer pays close attention to the larger significance of violence, beyond its connections to his notions of blackness. When covering the fight, he comments on the way that "boxing had shifted from speed and impact to the intimacy of movement. Delicately Ali would cradle Foreman's head with his left before he smashed it with his right" (205). Mailer's references to the "intimacy" of movement and the juxtaposition of Ali's seeming tenderness and brutality captures the difficult magnetism of boxing, the violence of which, to Mailer (and to writers like Oates as well), is not only magical but scientific, unique, and intricate; he says this fight in particular "bore serious resemblance to chess" (218).

Though Mailer respects the skill inherent in boxing, its violence is not, even in his mind, always worthy of glorification. Mailer makes its darker side apparent in "Ten Thousand Words a Minute," in which he also references the 1962 Benny Paret–Emile Griffith fight, in which Paret collapsed in the ring, fell into a coma, and died ten days later from a massive brain hemorrhage. Reflecting on the ripple effect of Paret's death on the culture of boxing, Mailer writes: "Gently, in thick, depressed hypocrisies, they tried to defend their sport. They did not find it easy to explain that they shared an unstated view of life which was religious. . . . It was an older religion, a more primitive one—a religion of blood, a murderous and sensitive religion."[13] After this, he says, "something in boxing was spoiled forever."[14]

Of course, this did not deter Mailer from further exploring the culture of boxing; he continued to write about and participate in the sport even after Paret's death. Mailer's comment does, however, show that he was cautiously invested in the sport. His commentary on Ali's win in *The Fight,* for instance, is tinged with concern, and with the sense that Ali's glory is transient. Mailer observes that, just before being declared the champion, Ali faints, a reaction that could be "the weakness of sudden exhaustion" or, perhaps, "a warning against excessive pride in years to come—one private bolt from Allah" (210). Mailer's reflections emphasize Ali's vulnerability and his humanity—he is not an invincible hero, but a man who is at the mercy of his own mortality and weakness. One of Mailer's final observations of Ali's humanity and flaws comes after observing him struggle to speak articulately to the press. At this moment,

Mailer writes: "With what an immensity of anxiety must Ali live at the size of his world role and his intimate knowledge of his own ignorance" (223). Thus, for all of the fascination and triumph that Mailer finds in boxing, for all of the potential magic that entices him, Mailer also acknowledges, with practicality but some sadness, that the sport also has its repercussions, the violence has its risk, the athletes their human faults.

Mailer continued to engage in a discussion of violence—albeit in a very different context—in *The Executioner's Song,* his Pulitzer Prize–winning account of the final months in the life of Gray Gilmore. In this meticulously researched piece of creative nonfiction, Mailer reconstructs the events leading up to Gilmore's murder of two innocent people in Utah, his subsequent trials and appeals, and Gilmore's turbulent ongoing relationship with Nicole Barrett.[15] The relationship with Barrett, as well as with other distant family, stands out most prominently in the first half of the book, titled "Western Voices." The second half, "Eastern Voices," chronicles the media circus surrounding Gilmore's trials and sentencing after the murders, and is largely seen through the eyes of Larry Schiller (who optioned the rights to Gary's life story, and then brought Mailer on board to write the book), as well as the lawyers involved in the case. Joan Didion famously pointed out the distinction between the narrative styles of these two parts, comparing them to "long symphonic movements." "Western Voices," Didion observes, features "voices which are most strongly voices of women," who "pass down stories," while the "Eastern Voices . . . are largely those of men—the voices of the lawyers, the prosecutors, the reporters, the people who move in the larger world and believe that they can influence events."[16] These gendered voices, as Didion eloquently points out, influence the tone of each of the book's two halves, the first being "a fatalistic drift, a tension, an overwhelming and passive rush toward the inevitable events that will end in Gary Gilmore's death" while the second is "the release of that tension, the resolution, the playing out of the execution, the active sequence."

Still, throughout the entire narrative, Mailer continually makes use of a simple, straightforward prose (which Didion called "a voice as flat as the horizon"), without the self-referential involvement that defined most of his earlier nonfictional works. In his appraisal of the relative absence of Mailer's authorial voice, Christopher Ricks points out, "The book promulgates no ideas or theories, though it contains a great many, as well as intelligent speculations, all voiced or thought by others."[17] Yet this alternative style does not mean that Mailer's influence and perspective have been entirely stripped from the text. As Mark Edmundson has suggested, Mailer is "alive" in *The Executioner's Song.* Though less visible than in his previous work, he is present in "the rhythmical shapings that he gives to the paragraphs."[18] Most significant, in Edmundson's view, is the way "we're led to associate Gary with a fall, with transgression," to believe that "Gilmore is fated, despite finer impulses, to fail" and that "his destiny is tragic." Such symbolism is certainly evident throughout the book, though it is not heavy-handed nor is it unquestioned. That is, though Mailer is clearly sympathetic to some aspects of Gilmore's character, and definitely intrigued by his intelligence and spiritual convictions, Gilmore is by no means painted as a hero who was simply a victim of fate. Though Mailer finds Gilmore intriguing and tragic, to interpret a glorification of his subject would be to overlook the complexity of *The Executioner's Song,* in which Mailer allows for ethical gray areas, unanswered questions, and the possibility that Gilmore might be a product of both unfortunate circumstance, and inexcusable, inexplicable choices.

We first meet Gary Gilmore in *The Executioner's Song* after he is released from prison on charges of armed robbery in 1976. His cousin Brenda Nicol has agreed to help him get back on his feet, with the hope that he will be able to rehabilitate himself among family in Provo, Utah. As she recalls, on the phone Gary "had a nice voice, soft spoken, twangy, held back. A lot of feeling in the center of it," a comment that immediately sets up the contradiction that Gary continued to perform: a gentle, emotive personality contrasted with that of a hardened criminal and, eventually, a cold-blooded killer (10). Adding to this initial impression, Mailer interprets their drive home from the prison as follows: "In the mountains, the snow was iron gray and purples in the hollows, and glowed like gold on every slope that faced the sun. The clouds over the mountains were lifting with light. Brenda took a good look into his eyes and felt full of sadness again. His eyes had the expression of rabbits she had flushed, scared-rabbit was the common expression, but she had looked into those eyes of scared rabbits and they were calm and tender and kind of curious. They did not know what would happen next" (16). Mailer emphasizes Gary's vulnerability and fear, painting him as a man who is "calm and tender" and thus, seemingly, fully capable of reform. His last line—that Gary's eyes "did not know what would happen next"—also suggests an instability, one that continues to escalate as the narrative progresses.

In fact, as Mailer recounts, Gilmore's family and friends' perceptions of him quickly become divided, as they begin to uncover the twin aspects of his personality. For instance, LuÁnn, a woman Gary briefly dates, says once, while speaking to him, she "felt his rage pass over her like a blast of air" (30), and Rikki Baker, Nicole's brother, "could see right off that Gary wasn't too honest" (38). Gary himself only exacerbates this mistrust and skepticism, even sometimes welcoming it, as he frequently confesses to people that he stabbed a man fifty-seven times in prison—a confession that many assumed to be dishonest braggadocio, but which is nevertheless unsettling. Yet Mont Court, his parole officer, says he "was able to see a part of the man simply not reflected in the prison record"; he "saw tenderness," particularly in Gary's artwork, and thought, "Gilmore can't be all evil, all bad. There's something that's salvageable" (53).

Nicole Baker Barrett, who begins a passionate relationship with Gary soon after they meet, is perhaps the only person in Gary's life who recognizes and embraces the conflicting sides of his personality. In Mailer's retelling, we can deduce that this acceptance is perhaps one of the reasons Gary is so drawn to her. Reconstructing Nicole's reflections on Gary, Mailer writes: "With her eyes closed, she had the odd feeling of an evil presence near her that came from Gary. She found it kind of half agreeable. Said to herself, Well, if he is the devil, maybe I want to get closer" (106). Nicole and Gary's relationship is passionate in every sense: they are candid and forthright about their sex life, both with one another, as evidenced by the letters they exchanged while Gary was in prison, and with others, as evidenced by interviews conducted by both Schiller and Mailer. Yet their relationship, at least so much as we are privy to it in *The Executioner's Song,* goes beyond the physical: they share a unique intimate bond that keeps drawing them back to one another.

Gary and Nicole also fight with equal passion: prior to his arrest, Gary is possessive of and aggressive with Nicole, particularly when he drinks. After a seemingly unending cycle of arguments and apologies, Nicole, who has two small children, decides to leave Gary. This sparks such an intense feeling in Gary—of both love for Nicole and hatred toward her—that he later says he killed Max Jensen and Benny Bushnell because "*I did not want to kill Nicole*" (691). Despite the chaos of their relationship (or, perhaps, as a symptom of it), Nicole continues to visit and write Gary in prison; in fact, according to Mailer's account, Gilmore's time in prison seems to only bring them closer, though their intimacy borders on self-destruction. Their sense of devotion reaches its height when they make a (failed) suicide pact while Gilmore is in jail, resulting in both of them being placed under close surveillance, barred from further visits.

While these relationships are arguably the central focus of *The Executioner's Song,* and are key to Mailer's exploration of the idiosyncrasies and dark corners of Gilmore's personality, Gilmore's murders of Benny Bushnell and Max Jensen remain the fulcrum around which the narrative turns. The account of these murders effectively ends Book 1, drawing the "Western Voices" to a close and making way for what Didion referred to as the released tension of the second half. Despite his attention to the ominous details that foreshadow

Gary's violence in the first half, and even though anyone reading *The Executioner's Song* would be well aware of the murders themselves, Mailer still manages to make these events seem surprising. This is, in part, because Mailer has hinted at the simmering potential of Gary's moral character, and has explained in detail his life with and love for Nicole. In the wake of the slowly building first half of the book, the murders read as Gilmore himself explained them: spontaneous, without premeditation. The result is that—as in a kind of horror movie, when the audience knows what is coming but does not know when—the reader is caught off guard by Gary's sudden and inexplicable violence. Though Mailer has provided some insight into Gary's character throughout the first half of the book, allowing us to offer some conjecture as to why he behaves as he does, here there seems to be no trace of that earlier, more vulnerable, deeply passionate Gary.

Mailer recounts the murders in a lucid, stripped-down style, which makes them more chilling but also enhances the sense of distance that Gary claims to feel from the violence. Of Max Jensen's murder, for example, Mailer simply writes: "[Gary] stood up. There was a lot of blood. It spread across the floor at a surprising rate. Some of it got onto the bottom of his pants" (224). Gary later says that the killings did not seem real to him, though he also confesses to Gibbs, his cellmate, that this claim is simply rhetoric—another detail that contributes to the indiscernible nature of his character. To whom is he lying? Mailer offers no firm answers. The cold-hearted, calculating Gary seems as convincing as the spiritual, intellectual, feeling Gary.

Certainly, the mysterious psychology of Gary Gilmore falls within the scope of Mailer's longstanding interests in psychopathy and violence. Mailer writes that, even though he could not be declared insane, Gary "did fit into a psychiatric category. . . . Psychiatrists called it 'psychopathic personality,' or, same thing, 'sociopathic personality.' It meant you were antisocial. In terms of accountability before the law, it was equal to sanity. The law saw a great difference between the psychotic and the psychopathic personality" (384). Such a commentary evokes Mailer's philosophy of the psychopathic personality explained in "The White Negro" (in fact, one of the earlier titles of *The Executioner's Song* was *The Saint and the Psychopath*), and thus one might assume Mailer would offer further commentary and insight into Gilmore's potential psychopathic tendencies. Here, however, he merely observes the diagnosis, maintaining the more removed authorial voice he has chosen for this particular work.

And in many ways, this seems only fitting: Gary's own confusing but undeniably intriguing personality seems to defy explanation or analysis. In Mailer's portrait, Gilmore continues to vacillate between being terrifying and sympathetic. Even on death row, he seems to garner equal amounts of rage and respect from those still involved in his life. When he is angry with Brenda for turning him in, Gary holds a grudge that disturbs her: she recalls that he "gave her a look that ate at her for a long time and never stopped bothering her" (446). Larry Schiller, who met with Gilmore four times to conduct interviews, says he could not shake the sense that Gary "could stick his knife in you and keep a smile while doing it" (620). Ron Stanger, Gary's lawyer, also senses this when listening to Gary spout angry racist comments during a phone conversation. At that moment, he thinks, "A dark side of Gilmore was running like a current into his ear. Man, he had an evil nature when he felt like it" (697).

Yet Noall Wootton, a prosecutor in Gary's case, is also struck by "the impression he had had all the way that Gilmore was more intelligent than himself," claiming that "'the system has really failed with this man, just miserably failed'" (447). Schiller, in addition to observing Gary's darker side, also observes Gary's magnetism, noting that, when making a point, he "spoke in the absolute confidence of the idea, spoke in the same quiet tone he might have employed if talking to only one man" (675). Additionally, Mailer himself takes care to emphasize that Gilmore is not only articulate and intelligent, but also spiritual and philosophical. Gary believes in karma and in reincarnation, and his spiritual life, in Mailer's account, deepens while he is incarcerated. To Nicole, for instance, Gary writes: "*When you die you will be free as never before in life—be able to travel at a tremendous speed just by thinking of some place you will be there. It's a natural thing and you adjust—it's just consciousness unencumbered by body*" (488). Later, also in a letter to Nicole, Gary writes: "*Once you asked me if I was the devil, remember? I'm not. The devil would be far more clever than I, would operate on a much larger scale and of course would feel no remorse. So I'm not Beelzebub. And I know the devil can't feel love. But I might be further from God than I am from the devil. Which is not a good thing*" (305). This is strikingly similar to Mailer's Manichean-Gnostic philosophy—that the earthly world is locked amid a battle between God and the devil, and that every individual exists on a spectrum between these two forces. Mailer was also vocal about his belief in karma; in a 1966 self-interview, "The Political Economy of Time," he offered an extended commentary on karma and the "metamorphoses of the soul," wherein he argues that the soul moves from one body to another by either "a literal or metaphorical leap."[19] Thus, perhaps, it is not surprising that even in this more removed writing style, Mailer's respect for Gilmore's own introspective, intellectual mysticism bleeds through.

The same qualities that attracted Mailer to Gilmore would, in fact, later draw him into his ill-fated relationship with Jack Abbott, with whom Mailer began a correspondence while working on *The Executioner's Song.* Mailer told

Abbott that his letters "lit up corners of [*Executioner*] that I might otherwise not have comprehended or seen only in the gloom of my instinct unfortified by experience."[20] Mailer agreed to write an introduction to Abbott's *In the Belly of the Beast,* in which he says that Abbott "has a mind like no other I have encountered" (xv), and he would later vouch for Abbott's parole in June 1981.[21] He would soon regret this, however, as just weeks after being released, Abbott murdered twenty-two-year-old waiter Richard Adan after Adan allegedly refused to allow Abbott to use the employee bathroom. Facing down public skepticism and backlash, however, Mailer continued to write to Abbott; in November 1982, he penned what he called "the toughest letter he had ever written" to Abbott, promising not to "sever relations."[22] Although he was horrified by Abbott's violence, Mailer also admitted that they had a "continuing psychological and emotional and spiritual relationship" that would last for life, and "perhaps beyond."[23]

In the end, Mailer's Gilmore embodies a similarly intriguing and unsettling paradox; he is a simultaneously magnetic and repulsive figure, whose character defies easy categorization. As Larry Schiller claims, Gary had the ability to perform "the kind of acting that makes you forget you are in a theater" (675). And because of this, it was difficult for many to determine where the acting ended and the real Gary began—if there were, in fact, such a distinction. As with Marilyn Monroe, as with the "otherness" of boxers like Ali and Foreman, it is this kind of unknowability and ongoing mystery that makes Gilmore such a compelling, if also disturbing, figure for Mailer and his reading public. After all, the America that watched the events of Gary's murders, convictions, and trials unfold was, like Mailer, caught in a vortex of fascination and revulsion. The gruesome murders and the sentence of the death penalty were enough to make headline news, but Gary's subsequent insistence that this penalty be carried out rather than appealed caused a media frenzy. As Mailer writes, "The public could live with a killer who was crazy, mixed-up, insane. But for a murderer to start controlling the issue—that was developing a lot of active hatred for Gilmore. People felt as if the world was being tipped on edge" (814). Ultimately, Gary does get his wish: executed in 1977, his last words were simply: "Let's do this." Mailer does not end the narrative here, however, but gives the last words to those characters he had also devoted so much time to shaping—to Gary's family, to his lawyers, to Nicole, to the producers of his story—all of whom were left to live in the wake of that execution. For while much of *The Executioner's Song* is Gary's story, it is also their story, and in a larger sense, it is also an American story: a story of American morals, American press, American reactions to tragedy. In this way, *The Executioner's Song* further exhibits what Midge Decter observed over a decade earlier: Mailer "owns America," and regardless of the subject, he is able to illuminate some central aspect of the American cultural identity.

Mailer's fixation on such indiscernible, contradictory, and violent figures continues to surface in his later work, and is especially evident in 1995's *Oswald's Tale: An American Mystery.* Here, Mailer delves into the mysterious life of Lee Harvey Oswald and the much-debated circumstances surrounding the events leading up to the assassination of President Kennedy. *Oswald's Tale* is another meticulously researched tome, also divided into two volumes: "Oswald in Minsk with Marina" and "Oswald in America." In the construction of both of these sections, Mailer relies on previously published studies of Oswald, particularly Priscilla Johnson Macmillan's *Marina and Lee.* In many ways, *Oswald's Tale* is also Marina's tale as well. Marina Oswald is herself a complex, interesting, and fiery figure, and Mailer (having interviewed her with Larry Schiller) relies heavily on her testimony and her memories of life with Oswald in the construction of narrative—though he is also careful to note the subjectivity and occasional shifting and evolution of her accounts over the years. To supplement Marina's intriguing but sometimes questionable testimony, Mailer also draws from previously unreleased KGB files on Oswald (to which Larry Schiller had gained access), as well as the Warren Commission Report. Yet while he offers a detailed account of the "facts" as they are presented and can be proven in such documents, he himself does not merely offer a straightforward report. Instead, much as he did in *Marilyn,* he strives to build his subject's life around and between the facts or "factoids," something he feels is particularly necessary in Oswald's case. As he writes, "A mystery of the immense dimensions of Oswald's case will, in the writing, create a form of its own somewhere between fiction and non-fiction" (353).

Moreover, though Mailer explores the various conspiracy theories surrounding the assassination, he does not land on any one of these as more or less probable. As he says, "Evidence, by itself, will never provide the answer to a mystery. For it is in the nature of evidence to produce, sooner or later, a counterinterpretation to itself. . . . one does not (and should not) respect evidence with the religious intensity that others bring to it"—a comment that also echoes his opinions about the dangerous nature of "factoids" surrounding the life of Marilyn Monroe (775). Mailer makes it clear that in writing *Oswald's Tale* his aim is not to solve a mystery, or prove or disprove popularized theories about the assassination. As he says of his time conducting interviews and research in Russia, "the task . . . had not been to look for such an answer. . . . this was not a search for a smoking gun. . . . it was more one's aim . . . to set up a base camp on the slopes of such a mystery" (349).

The first half of *Oswald's Tale,* "Oswald in Minsk," is written in clear, clipped language, meant to imitate a Russian-inflected English that would contribute to the general ambiance of that period in Oswald's life. (Mailer states in his preface to the book, however, that he did not offer a "full effort in that direction" as he believes it would likely have "tortured the English language beyond repair.") In this section, Mailer's Oswald, who first appears to us upon his arrival in Russia at the age of twenty, is presented as a largely pathetic, naive figure—dissatisfied, confused, moody, and fickle. Barely out of his teens, he decides to denounce the United States and move to the USSR; however, after passionate pleas to be accepted as a Russian citizen, extensive bureaucratic red tape, and extended KGB surveillance, Oswald questions whether he truly wants to commit himself to a life in Russia. Moreover, he refuses to devote himself to becoming fluent in Russian, he does not explore the city or its environs, and though he finds a job, his colleagues describe him as lazy, arrogant, and disrespectful.

Despite these multiple accounts of Oswald from a number of acquaintances in Russia, as well as the KGB surveillance files which track his every movement for months, Oswald remains an elusive character. Mailer even admits this detailed portrait of Oswald cannot help but leave an air of ambiguity surrounding Oswald's personality. This is in part because the banality of his life and character seems to stand in such a contrast to the act for which he later becomes infamous, and because we are never privy to his interior thoughts. While Mailer argues that there is "no doubt" that Oswald was a secret agent, he also states that what remains mysterious "is whether he was working for any service larger than the power centers in the privacy of his mind" (352). As Mailer predicted, we are left with more questions than answers even after the book's first half: what could have inspired Oswald to become so disillusioned with the United States that he would defect to Russia? What might he have been running from?

One of the possibilities Mailer puts forth is that Oswald was driven away by certain uniquely American pressures of manhood. In fact, his study of Oswald itself becomes, in part, a study of the struggle to be a man in an American society that had very particular, very complex, and very burdensome notions of what a "real" American man should be. Mailer suggests that Oswald, influenced by the ideals of masculinity enforced during the 1950s, believed he must earn his way into manhood, that he must be "bold, forthright, competitive, individual, courageous, and innovative," and initially, Oswald saw the Marine Corps as his way into this manhood (369). As Mailer further explains, "The Marine Corps laid it out for you: your ability with an M-1 was equal to your virility—there was no reason to be in the Marine Corps if virility was not the center of your focus" (381). In other words, Oswald has also been instructed that violence is and should be intricately interwoven into his masculine identity. If he fails to be assertive, aggressive, and skilled with his weapon, he risks being feminized and emasculated.

This, Mailer theorizes, may have been particularly fearsome to Oswald in light of rumors of his sexual fluidity—also considered unacceptable to American masculinity at the time. "Indeed," Mailer continues, "his young life is a study in one recurring theme—I am not yet a man and I must become one—which in the late Fifties and early Sixties became a compelling motif for many young men terrified by homosexual inclinations and ready to go to great lengths to combat and/or conceal them." At the time, Mailer observes, homosexuality was considered "one of those omnibus infections of the spirit that could lead to God knows what further aberration" (379). In fact, as he also argues with a subtly critical tone, "the Warren Commission came to the unvoiced conclusion that it might be all for the best if Oswald turned out to be homosexual. That would have the advantage of explaining much even if it explained nothing at all" (379).

In addition to emphasizing the role that Oswald's threatened sense of masculine identity may have played in his actions, Mailer also examines what he sees to be Oswald's twin qualities of insecurity and narcissism. He proposes the likelihood that Oswald acted alone in his assassination of JFK out of a misguided desire for recognition, so that his life might mean something. To make his mark, Mailer theorizes, Oswald felt he needed to change the political system with which he was so dissatisfied, and which he felt was destroying America. As he writes, "In the profoundest sense, as Oswald saw it, he had located the tumor—it was that Kennedy was too good. The world was in crisis and the social need was to create conditions for recognizing that there had to be a new kind of society. . . . An explosion at the heart of the American establishment's complacency would be exactly the shock therapy needed to awaken the world" (781).

This impetus for Oswald's action in particular is something with which Mailer himself struggles, for more than one reason. Mailer, while exuding praise for and hope in Kennedy, had expressed dissatisfaction with American complacency throughout his career, so in this sense his views are aligned with those assigned to Oswald. Additionally, as a man concerned with his own literary legacy, he understands the impulse to leave a mark on society. At the same, time, Mailer also recognizes the flawed reasoning that might lead the American public—himself included—to grant that significance to Oswald, thus handing him exactly what he had wanted. As he writes, "So long as Oswald is a petty figure, [a] lone twisted pathetic killer who happened to be in a position to kill a potentially great President, then . . . America is cursed with an absurdity. There was no logic to the event and no sense of balance in the universe . . . If a figure as large as Kennedy is cheated abruptly of his life, we feel better, inexplicably better, if his killer is also not without size. Then, to some degree, we can also mourn the loss of possibility in the man who did the deed. Tragedy is vastly preferable to absurdity" (606–7). In other words, for many Americans, to acknowledge that there was nothing special about Oswald would be to somehow diminish Kennedy's death. It is more comforting, Mailer suggests, to believe that only a man of equal (if more terrible) greatness could take Kennedy's life so quickly.

Despite his acknowledgment of this dilemma, Mailer's own portrait of Oswald does suggest that the latter *is* in fact a petty figure, thus implying that America is in a sense "cursed with an absurdity" that cannot be explained. Mark Olshaker argues that the "petty" nature so emphasized in *Oswald's Tale* is why that particular life study, in spite of its perennially fascinating subject, is not as deeply affective as *The Executioner's Song.* The problem, Olshaker suggests, is that "Oswald's small and tawdry life does not lend itself to large questions, as does Gary Gilmore's equally sordid but more interesting and intellectually challenging existence."[24]

Nevertheless, some have read into Mailer's book an attempt to recuperate Oswald's reputation, or at least to use him as an example of the kind of violent individualism that Mailer explores in his earlier work. For example, Barrie Balter claims that Mailer wants to fashion Oswald into an "everyman" (136) and argues that "Mailer reads Oswald's crime as an Emersonian act of self-making—both audacious and peculiarly American," one that makes him "both villain and hero."[25] While there may be ambivalence at the center of Mailer's portrait, nothing about Oswald is represented as triumphant or heroic. If he is "peculiarly American," he largely represents America's faults: a need for fame and celebrity, a distinct ennui, arrogance, and entitlement. While Mailer recognizes the desire to make something formidable out of Oswald, he also recognizes there is simply not enough evidence to do so. Though Oswald has the hint of the rebel in him that Mailer might normally admire, ultimately his rebellion is not productive, but destructive. In fact, one might argue that Oswald inspires Mailer to revise the more glorifying claims about violence that he espoused earlier in his career, particularly in works like "The White Negro." For in *Oswald's Tale,* he concludes, "The murderer kills in order to cure himself—which is why murder is properly repudiated. It is the most selfish of acts" (781).

In the same year Mailer published *Oswald's Tale,* he also released a biographical study of a very different figure: Pablo Picasso. In *Portrait of Picasso as a Young*

Man: An Interpretive Biography, Mailer attempts to make sense of the life of a painter he deems "the artist who came to signify the dislocations and horrendous metamorphoses of the prodigious century to come" (34). This book was not the first indication of Mailer's interest in Picasso: in *Advertisements for Myself,* he included a short piece called "An Eye on Picasso" and had also planned to pen a biography of Picasso as early as 1962 but eventually shelved the project. It is also unsurprising that Mailer would devote a book-length work to the artist, since Mailer himself also dabbled in the visual arts, producing a number of sketches that invoke a Modernist aesthetic in their relative abstraction.[26] Moreover, in a 1985 interview, Mailer would assert, "The twentieth-century artist who conceivably had the most influence on my work was not a writer but Picasso" for "he kept changing the nature of his attack on reality."[27]

In *Portrait of Picasso,* finally published in 1995, Mailer blends facts and insight to shape his subject, using his own experience as a writer and artist over the years to inform his biographical study. His own involvement as narrator here lies somewhere between that found in *The Fight,* wherein he makes himself a primary player, and *The Executioner's Song,* where he keeps himself firmly at a distance. In *Picasso,* Mailer also draws heavily from a number of previously published biographies (as he did with *Oswald's Tale*), including *Picasso and His Friends* by Fernande Olivier, one of Picasso's mistresses (whose memoir Mailer also translated from the original French), and *Picasso: Creator and Destroyer* by Arianna Huffington, as well as Gertrude Stein's *Autobiography of Alice B. Toklas.* He himself admits to this heavy reliance on others in his preface, claiming to offer "no original scholarship" (something that disappointed some critics), emphasizing instead that his aim here is to arrive at an "individual understanding" of the painter (xii).

In order to arrive at such an understanding, Mailer explores several different aspects of Picasso's character, though he is perhaps most concerned with Picasso's ego and his love life—two aspects that feature prominently in the artist's work. According to Mailer's narrative, Picasso's sense of self and his sexual life are intricately intertwined, so that it becomes largely unsurprising that the teenage Picasso who would sign paintings with the phrase "I, the King," becomes the man who "would always be ready to certify the legend that he had always been a voraciously active sexual animal" (67). The role of sex in art—not to mention its relevance to a sense of masculine selfhood—is a topic on which Mailer is well versed, and here lies one element of his affinity for and identification with Picasso.[28] On the subject of ego in Picasso's life and work, Mailer is similarly empathetic, noting that it is "not uncommon for writers, actors, or painters to be narcissists" which can be "handmaiden to one's art" but can also cause an "intolerable sense of self-imprisonment" (149).

Relatedly, Mailer is aware of and sympathetic to Picasso's fraught relationship with the women in his life. Picasso, as Mailer recounts, became infatuated with a number of his mistresses, yet the significance he lent to them (and to their opinions of him) also threatened his ego and sense of masculinity. Picasso loves women, but as Mailer suggests, Picasso also saw women as "harbingers of mortal threat" (67) and argues that "there is little question that in this period, one drawing after another is there to remind us of the impotence of the male and the overbearing carnal presence of the female" (66). Mailer also observes, "No man ever loved and hated women more" (356); as he further explains: "We ought to know that violence and creativity all too often connect themselves inextricably . . . and so in maturity, love is frequently followed by hate, and creation by destruction. So were Picasso's illimitable powers of insight locked into a powerfully negative view of the permanence of all tender sentiments" (352).

Sometimes, one is left to wonder whether Mailer allots Picasso too much sympathy with regard to his affairs with women. On the fact that Picasso slept with his friend Casagemas's widow after Casagemas committed suicide, for instance, Mailer writes: "If, in the process, he became the dead man's sexual overlord and (to put it at its worst and most extreme) the thief of Casagemas' romantic hopes beyond the grave, it was also an act of love. . . . to fornicate with Germaine was to invoke Casagemas rather than to dispel him" (53). While theories like these are certainly interesting in their evocation of the kind of mysticism that attracted Mailer throughout his career, they are also highly questionable—the most subjectively speculative aspects of the interpretive biography. Mailer makes no secret of his intention to rehabilitate part of Picasso's reputation, however. "If he has often been depicted as a monster in his relations with women," Mailer writes, "let him also be characterized as wholly magnetized by such relationships" (94).

To examine this magnetism, Mailer makes room to explore the lives of the women in Picasso's life as well: in the same way that Marina became an equally intriguing focus in *Oswald's Tale,* the women in Picasso's life become as central to *Portrait of Picasso as a Young Man* as the painter himself. Mailer is particularly fascinated with Fernande Olivier, one of "seven major mistresses and wives who would exercise a measurable influence upon his work" (94). Fernande, he argues, "will prove by turns piquant and banal, vain and wounded, critical and generous, wise and full of folly" (111). Mailer appreciates the complexity of her character, and the mystery of her unhappiness and inability to find love—something with which he also concerns himself in *Marilyn.*

Reviewers did not take too kindly to *Portrait of Picasso*; as Mailer lamented, the book was "gang banged" by the critics.[29] Michiko Kakutani, notorious for her consistently negative reviews of most of Mailer's work, argues that the book is "less a real biography than an assemblage of other people's words, glued together with Mr. Mailer's own musings and speculation." In the same review, however, Kakutani offers a concise and insightful summary of why Picasso was such a fascinating subject for Mailer, observing how this work fits with relative ease into Mailer's existing canon. As Kakutani writes:

> "It's easy to understand why Norman Mailer would want to write a biography of Picasso. The painter, after all, can be seen as a kind of artistic role model for Mr. Mailer. . . . Both have been chameleons throughout their career, shrugging on and off a multitude of artistic styles with fluency and ease. Both have made very public inventories of their psyches, using their own obsessions as a kind of index to a tumultuous world, even as they've dramatized themselves as outlaws. And both have enshrined art as a magical, shamanistic force, offering the possibility of exorcism and transformation."[30]

While this particular book may lack the originality and unique voice of Mailer's other interpretive biographies, it does—as Kakutani herself points out—tap into the themes and obsessions that recur throughout Mailer's canon: public identity, the glorification of the outlaw, the power of magic, a battle with internal demons, and the possibility of redemption.

CHAPTER 6

The Divided Self across Genre

Novels of the 1980s and 1990s

During the 1980s and 1990s, Mailer continued to experiment with a variety of narrative styles, publishing works that ranged from an epic tale of Ancient Egypt (1983's *Ancient Evenings*), a murder mystery (1984's *Tough Guys Don't Dance*), a meticulously researched CIA novel (1991's *Harlot's Ghost*), and a novella that reimagines the life of Jesus, written in a language imitative of the Christian New Testament (1997's *The Gospel According to the Son*). While these novels vary widely in many respects, they are linked by at least one common concern: the nature of psychological contradiction and paradox. Part of Mailer's aim in each of these texts, whether he is exploring ancient Egyptian myth or Christian theology, is to reflect upon the conundrums we face when forced to contend with competing perspectives, ideologies, and impulses. Moreover, each of these novels reckons with the power of theology and mysticism in the construction of such internal and external dualities, exhibiting Mailer's ongoing interest in the influence of the spiritual and mystical aspects of the world.

A number of individuals, including Mailer himself, have referred to *Ancient Evenings* as his "magnum opus."[1] On some grounds, a case can be made for this assertion: Mailer not only spent ten years working on the 709-page novel, but the published work also contains reflections on nearly all of the ideas with which he had been preoccupied for the duration of his career to that point. The novel, like a good portion of Mailer's work, received mixed reviews, but this particular book left critics more baffled than the others did, perhaps because its style, scope, and setting depart so drastically from Mailer's earlier work.

Harold Bloom, for instance, wrote that "our most conspicuous literary energy has generated its weirdest text, a book that defies usual aesthetic standards, even as it is beyond the conventional ideas of good and evil."[2] Mailer himself called it his "most ambitious book" as well as his "most unusual," and says that he chose to write about Egypt because it was "one of the places where magic was being converted into social equivalence."[3]

By delving into the history, religion, and culture of Ancient Egypt, Mailer is able to thoroughly explore concepts of reincarnation, mysticism, and magic, situating these explorations within a historical context in which such ideas might be seen as more "acceptable" than in a more conservative, contemporary Western culture. In other words, the setting of this novel allows him more freedom to probe such topics more deeply, as it provides a necessary distance from a more skeptical or cynical modern society. As Robert Begiebing observed in what is arguably the most in-depth and insightful analysis of this difficult work, "Mailer found in Egypt . . . an extremely fertile ground in which to plant and let flourish his fascination with the way extraordinary people have acted out and often failed in the eternal drama of the soul's struggle for 'salvation' through the ancient patterns of rebirth."[4] After all, Ancient Egypt is, for many, a mythical era—far from the realm of familiar contemporary understanding, and knowable primarily through the art and artifacts obtained through archeological and anthropological study. Mailer's goal in *Ancient Evenings* is to breathe life into such a culture, retaining some of its mythical qualities while also illuminating the humanity and corporeality of its characters.

The novel is largely a story within a story: during the reign of Ramses the Ninth, a nobleman named Menenhetet, renowned throughout the kingdom for purportedly having been reincarnated three times, is invited by the pharaoh to narrate the stories of his previous lives. *Ancient Evenings* predominantly encompasses the lengthy story of his life as advisor to Ramses the Second. "My story must be long like the length of the snake," he says. "If I present the head, you will know nothing of the body. Only the smile of the snake" (228). Here one might read Menenhetet's justification for the duration of his tale as Mailer's as well, for *Ancient Evenings* is a hefty tome, in which Mailer spares no detail. By crafting Menenhetet's life story in such an intricate fashion, Mailer weaves a rich tapestry of history, myth, violence, warfare, political strife, and—perhaps most pointedly—the mystical power of sex.

While meditations on sex factor into nearly all of Mailer's works, this subject lies at the very heart of *Ancient Evenings,* functioning as the novel's thematic lynchpin. Mailer emphasizes repeatedly throughout the novel that sexual organs and the act of sex itself are the seats of power, both for the gods (as he retells the myth of Isis and Osiris at the beginning of the novel), as well for the gods in human form (such as the pharaohs), and even for the humble servants and human subjects in Egypt. The novel opens with a scene in which the Ka (or spirit) of Menenhetet "One" meets his reincarnated self, Menenhetet Two. The meeting is, like most encounters in the novel, highly sexualized. For example, Menenhetet Two describes how this meeting arouses him in a wholly unfamiliar way. "My belly was as sentimental as a flower, and my buttocks in honey," he says. "I had never felt so agreeable before. Was this the power and pleasure of a woman? Whatever had become of my pride in a phallus as dependable as my arm?" (70). Menenhetet is baffled by his arousal in the face of meeting not just another man, but another version of himself—and thus we are ushered into the bizarre eroticized world that, while based in history, is very much of Mailer's making.

The homoeroticism that Mailer begins to explore early in the novel continues throughout, as he reveals a keen interest in exploring desires that exist outside of contemporary heteronormative standards. He muses on the pleasure, shame, denial, and acceptance men feel in exploring these desires, inviting the reader into the internal conflict and divided sentiments of his characters. For example, as Menenhetet Two notes after the encounter with his Ka: "It used to be legitimate, if a filthy habit, to jam the force of one's own cock in to the ass of any friend (or enemy) weak enough to take it, a way of measuring ourselves, but nonetheless! every mark of a noble Egyptian was his detestation of such dirt" (70). That is, while practiced as a form of dominance (and likely for pleasure as well), the sodomy Menenhetet describes is fraught with masculine anxiety, inciting a sort of paradox: the very thing that is used to enforce masculine power is also what emasculates men.

Thus, even in the more sexually flexible world Mailer imagines, men are still constricted by their own need to adhere to such heteronormative standards. As Joseph Allen Boone has observed, the sexual tension between men in the novel "signals a threshold or boundary whose transgression threatens to dissolve a world based on the phallus, dominance, and gender hierarchy."[5] Boone goes on to note that "the homoerotic fantasies unleashed by and legitimated in *Ancient Evenings'* structural and thematic celebration of the polymorphous perverse, then, generates a crisis of masculine subjectivity" which in turn "compels Mailer to Promethean efforts to contain the very desires upon which his exploration of ancient Egypt's otherness has depended."[6] While Mailer certainly explores the degrees of guilt and shame that the "polymorphous perverse" brings to his male characters, to say he seeks to "contain it" is debatable. Rather, it might be more accurate to say that he seeks to manipulate such desire so that it can exist openly, but also fits within his own society's current notion of dominant masculinity—hence his discussion of it as a means of asserting power.[7]

Moreover, the fraught nature of sexuality and desire in the novel can be seen as Mailer's way of interrogating the constricting nature of masculinity, rather than participating in the constraint of that desire himself. For example, consider the development of the complex relationship between Meni and Ramses II. After a sexual encounter with the pharaoh, Menenhetet says, "I was no longer myself but His, and loved Him, and knew I would die for Him, but I also knew I would never forgive Him" (279). Meni feels humiliated that Ramses II has "measured himself" against him and exerted his sexual power over him, yet he also feels that, by sodomizing him, Ramses II has passed on to him strength and sexual potency. Meni also talks about the deep, homosocial bond he shares with the pharaoh, one that is not as directly sexual, though still sexually inflected. Once, for instance, when a harem of "little queens" is pleasuring the pharaoh, Ramses holds Menenhetet's hand, and Meni says, "I was able to know Him in those moments as none who is not a Pharaoh can ever know so Good and Great a God" (409–10).

Problematically, however, Menenhetet then uses the power he feels is transferred to him by the pharaoh to sodomize other men: in one instance, he describes leaving a victim "sobbing on the ground, grateful for the tenth time that he was not dead" and "mourning in himself all of those qualities he would never know again" (298)—for those qualities have been transferred to Menenhetet, just as Ramses II transferred some of his own power to Meni during their own sexual encounter. Here, one cannot help but think of the sexual tension that exists between Shago Martin and Stephen Rojack in *An American Dream*, where Rojack notes that "violence seemed to shake himself free from [Shago] every time I smashed him back to the floor and shake itself into me" (193). For Menenhetet, sex poses the possibility of redemption and power—as it also does for a contemporary character like Rojack.

Moreover, sex becomes a determining factor with regard to who Menenhetet will be in his next life; in fact, it becomes the focus around which Menenhetet gauges his many lives. As he says, "As a cause of all the fears with which I made love the last time, yet by virtue of the audacity of the venture, my second life became the highest compromise of my ambitions" (635). Thus, he practices the art of lovemaking during his second life so that, at the end, "all that was gross in me fell back into the ruins of my body, but my seed was sent across the bridge, and that seed, I hope, was not like me, but finer. I believe we have the power, when unhappy with ourselves, to prepare a few virtues we do not possess and pass them to our seed" (659). This, too, echoes Rojack's belief in the power of his "seed," when he has sex with both Ruta and with Cherry. Menenhetet also talks about climbing temple walls, testing his courage in much the same way Rojack does when circling the parapet—a trope that also appears in

Mailer's next novel, *Tough Guys Don't Dance,* as well as 1991's *Harlot's Ghost.* "I felt closer to Geb holding myself to these wrinkles in His rocky skin than I had known you could come to a God without prayer," Menenhetet says about his climb (277). Mailer himself admits that he walked around parapets to test his own courage; "I felt as if it was an imperative from my soul to take such a chance," he says in *On God* (125). As evidence of the ways in which Mailer's own contemporary concerns find their way into *Ancient Evenings,* these similarities allow us to draw a connecting thread across Mailer's divergent works in order to see the ways in which he experiments with different iterations of his abiding thematic concerns.

Some critics found the placement of such modern concerns in a text about Ancient Egypt disorienting and problematic. For example, Benjamin DeMott writes in the *New York Times* that one of the problems with the book is that "the mentality of the dynastic world, magically imagined in the book's opening pages, is replaced with fearful abruptness by the preoccupations and obsessions of a late 20th century mind—Norman Mailer's—as soon as the narrator settles into his dinner party discourse."[8] Anthony Burgess similarly points to Mailer's preoccupation with modern rather than ancient Egyptian concerns as one of the flaws of the novel.[9] On the other hand, Ashton Howley argues that *Ancient Evenings* does, in fact, reflect "the era in which it is set," but that ultimately "Mailer's achievement is to delineate, consciously or otherwise, an earlier imperial culture as a mirroring image of our present global one."[10] Mailer himself would likely take issue with such readings; in fact, he said he thinks he will "have failed" if people start reading the book with the idea that the novel would "teach us something about today" (327). Instead, he says, the attraction of the novel is in its "lack of connection" (328). While this may be a reflection of his personal intentions, the echo of more contemporary concerns (even if unintentional) need not be considered a failure. That is, while Mailer may indeed be funneling modern gendered preoccupations through his Egyptian narrative, and while some readers might find these moves anachronistic, such preoccupations also work to bring Egypt to life and humanize its characters. While the setting remains foreign and intriguingly mystical, figures like Ramses II and Menenhetet are more three-dimensional as a result of their anxieties and personal struggles.

While the power of sex and sexual desire lies at the center of the book, Mailer is also fixated on the power of the body in general, specifically bodily fluids and waste, which become part of the larger position of magic and mysticism in the everyday lives of the characters. For example, at one point, Ramses explains: "Each morning, you see, I had told Myself that whatever in Me was failing to serve the interests of the Two-Lands, whatever I might lack in dedication, piety, raw bravery, and martial spirit—for alas, I am a prudent man—were, nonetheless, all present in My stool" (213). Therefore, he explains, he would put his stool in the garden to be used as fertilizer, and would then give the vegetables that grew to his most trusted advisors. Such a philosophy invokes some of Mailer's own earlier writings—specifically, "The Metaphysics of the Belly," in which he theorizes that we "excrete not only what we despise but what is too good for us as well" because "feces are the material evidence of the processes of communication within us."[11]

Ancient Evenings, however, is more than a story about the sexuality and corporeality of its subjects; it is also a story about the power of narrative, specifically, the human need for storytelling and for myth. Ramses IX, for example, is frequently unnerved and even angry when parts of Menenhetet's story do not match up with his own understanding of history, and is pleased when they do—not only because it suggests his own powers of vision as a pharaoh, but also because it shows that he who has the language, the history, and the knowledge holds the power. As Richard Poirier notes, "The telling and listening have less to do with a desire to get somewhere . . . but rather to get away from the loneliness, darkness, waste and dissolution which are, interestingly enough, the conditions Mailer has worried about since the mid-1950s as peculiar to the fate of the writer, especially the American writer, in the last half of the century."[12] Moreover, the name Menenhetet, as Christopher Ricks points out, means "Foundation-of-speech," and Meni (like Mailer) is fascinated with the nuances of Egyptian language and writing, wherein one symbol can have two entirely divergent meanings.[13] Egyptians, as Menenhetet himself points out, will "turn a word into the opposite of itself" (479). Thus, in addition to the internal duality represented by the characters' gendered and sexual conflicts, the complex mythology and oral histories that make up *Ancient Evenings* indicate Mailer's fascination with the duality embedded in language itself.

Tough Guys Don't Dance, written and released just a year after the publication of *Ancient Evenings,* is, in style, genre, and plot, incredibly different from that previous novel. *Tough Guys* exemplifies Mailer's foray into a campy murder mystery, marked with the kind of eerie magic and dark existential dread that has come to define much of Mailer's work. Mailer makes Provincetown, Massachusetts, the backdrop of this novel, and the setting effectively becomes a character in and of itself, lending a Gothic-Romantic impression to the narrative and contributing to the aura of mystery that surrounds the tale. "There could be no other town like it," protagonist Tim Madden says of Provincetown. "Conceived at night (for one would swear it was created in the course of one dark storm) its sand flats still glistened in the dawn with the moist primeval innocence of land exposing itself to the sun for the first time" (7–8). He describes the town as haunted, particularly by a "spiritual vengeance" (59), enforced by those who had died decades before in "Hell-Town," the area's former shady underbelly; as a result, "something of a perished Klondike of whores and smugglers, and whalers with wages hot in their pockets, lived in our walls" (64).

It is against this scene that Mailer introduces us to Madden, a struggling writer and former Golden Gloves boxer who claims that his proudest moment occurred when he was able to sleep with a woman six minutes after meeting her. Madden wakes up one morning to find blood on the seat of his car, a decapitated head among his marijuana stash in the woods, and no memory of the night before. Realizing he is the prime suspect in the murder of Jessica Pond, a visitor to Provincetown with whom he had spent the previous night, Madden sets out to retrace his steps and recover his memory. What follows is a noir-tinged exploration of the darker corners of Provincetown and its cast of characters, who, as James Emmett Ryan aptly notes, "provide a living theater for the collapse of moral and social categories that Mailer implicitly suggests."[14] The cast of characters includes his wife, Patty Lareine; Patty's ex-husband Wardley Meeks; Madden's ex-wife Madeleine; corrupt policeman Alvin Luther Regency, to whom Madeleine is now married; a local barfly named Spider; Spider's eccentric girlfriend and his accomplice "Stoodie"; and Madden's own father. Though we are offered some insight into the backgrounds of these characters, our knowledge of them is limited, for in *Tough Guys* Mailer narrows his point of view—another notable departure from *Ancient Evenings*. Though Mailer employed first-person perspective in *Ancient Evenings* though the character of Meni, he did so through a structure of layered narratives, offering Meni such hindsight over his past lives that the character was granted a kind of omniscience. In *Tough Guys,* however, we are privy only to the views of Tim Madden, and thus experience the mystifying chain of events as Madden does.

Throughout the novel, Madden's recollections of events and interactions with these characters often serve to raise more questions than answers, resulting in a convoluted plot that comes to a rushed conclusion. Adding to the confusion is Madden's status as an unreliable narrator, confessing from the start that his "memory is damnable" (24) and going on to say, "My dreams were now as reasonable as my memory, or my memory was as untrustworthy as my dreams. In either event, I could not tell them apart" (37). Such a strategy forces us to second-guess all clues provided in the first half of the novel, exhibiting Mailer's deftness for creating suspense—though as many critics have observed, the suspense does not quite pay off. Mailer himself called the book "the weakest" of his novels, an "example of what happens when you have to do what is necessary" in order to pay the bills.[15]

Moreover, Denis Donoghue has also argued that there is little originality in or depth to the character of Tim Madden, who he says "merely brings together the already well-documented sequence of Mailer's obsessions."[16] Madden is, admittedly, quite similar to Stephen Rojack of *An American Dream* in a number of ways.[17] Madden, like Rojack, exists in a state of existential dread, unsure not only of his future but of his sanity. "I had to recognize I was not automatically sane," he admits at one point (100), later noting that "there is this to be said for madness: your blood can pass from one transcendental moment to another without fear" (244). Such admissions also invoke Rojack's reflections at the beginning of *An American Dream,* wherein he feels he is about to slip the lip of sanity unless he faces and transcends his existential crisis. Additionally, Madden's wife, Patty, leaves him for a black man named Bolo, which arouses in him oppositional feelings of animosity and admiration, as he cites a "carnal affinity toward black men which lives in the hearts of certain blondes like lightning and thunder"—an idea that seems to allude to Rojack's feelings about Cherry Melanie's relationship with Shago Martin (40). He also writes that it delighted Patty's "contempt" that he "was not man enough" to simply shoot her black lover. As he says: "I would indeed get my gun, but never to chase Mr. Black. He was just appropriating what I, too, would grab if I could fill his jockstrap and sweat properly in his black logic. No, I was afraid I would get my pistol and never leave the house before emptying a magazine into her all-superior fuck-you face" (40).

Thus, the novel clearly encompasses Mailer's ongoing fixation upon the performance of masculinity, racialized masculinities, and the sexual anxieties that drive masculine crises. Like many of Mailer's previous works, it is sometimes difficult to tell whether Mailer is endorsing or sending up his protagonists' hypermasculine personas. As Scott Duguid argues, the book "clearly has a lot of fun with Mailer's own macho image . . . yet, reading the novel, one is often reminded of Kate Millett's early feminist assertion that 'he always seems to understand what's the matter with masculine arrogance, but he can't give it up.'"[18]

Tough Guys bears similarities to other works as well: Madden's boxing history recalls that of Sergius O'Shaughnessy in *The Deer Park* (as well as Rojack's); his attempt to climb the walls of the Provincetown monument is reminiscent not just of Rojack's attempt to circle the parapet of Barney Oswald Kelly's high-rise, but also of Ramses II's achievement in climbing a "pinnacle of stone" in *Ancient Evenings* as proof of his power. Additionally, volatile detective Alvin Luther Regency embodies the cop/criminal duality that Mailer explored in his experimental film *Beyond the Law*: as Madden himself states, "a man becomes a cop to be shielded from his own criminality" (344). Mailer's ideas about cancer also make their way into the book via Madden's father, who says that, when he gave up chasing a man who had shot him to seek help at a nearby hospital instead, he "felt the first switch get thrown in the cancer" which then developed after "forty-five years of living with no respect for myself" (258). Though Madden claims to believe this is nonsense, he is compelled by his father's ensuing argument that "schizophrenics in loony bins only get cancer half as often as the average population. I figure it this way: either your body goes crazy, or your mind" (258). Such a comment invokes Mailer's own theory, which he began developing early in his career, and continued to hone throughout his life. "It's *not* living in courageous moments that gives one cancer," Mailer once said. "One of the causes of cancer must be absence of action."[19]

Mailer would later write and direct the film adaptation of *Tough Guys Don't Dance* as well. Released in 1987 and starring Ryan O'Neal and Isabella Rosellini, the film received some mixed reviews that veered more towards the negative than the positive, and it did not fare well at the box office. At this point in his career, Mailer had a keen sense of humor about such reviews: for instance, he created a trailer for *Tough Guys Don't Dance* in which he is featured reading the diametrically opposed reviews of the film—a strategy he also used when advertising his earlier experimental films, as well as novels like *The Deer Park* and *Marilyn*. Though the movie was filmed in Provincetown and boasted some impressive cinematography (thus echoing the achievements of the book as well, whose setting is arguably its strongest element), its tone is so uneven that even deeming it "camp" cannot quite explain its unintentionally comedic scenes, which prevent the serious appraisal of the town and its characters that the book does invite.[20] The faltering film adaptation aside, *Tough Guys Don't Dance*—though a shorter, more hastily written, perhaps more "generic" work—is arguably as much an encapsulation of Mailer's ideological preoccupations as is *Ancient Evenings*. It is as though Mailer has used this book as a way to pause and collect his thoughts before embarking on his next project: 1991's more detailed, in-depth researched, spy thriller, *Harlot's Ghost*.

Harlot's Ghost opens as protagonist Harry Hubbard, formerly a CIA undercover operative, is fleeing to Russia, in fear for his life; with him he carries a manuscript documenting the highly classified activities in which he was engaged throughout his career. After this opening scene, the novel jumps back in time, tracking these activities, as well as Harry Hubbard's personal life, as he travels from Berlin to Washington to Montevideo to Miami, chronicling the peaks and nadirs of Hubbard's intriguing but ultimately disappointing career that spans everything from the Cold War to Watergate. As Harry states, the CIA was "a company of the elegant, secretly gathered to fight a war so noble that one could and must be ready to trudge for years throughout the mud and the pits" (167). Unfortunately for Harry, much of his tenure at the organization involves trudging through "the mud and the pits," without the reward of much prestige; as he says, later in his career he was treated as one of the "*sad people,*" which is "equal to being an unproductive child in a large and talented family" (31).

Mailer was quick to admit that this novel was a work of fiction, but also noted that it was "the product of a veteran imagination that has pondered the ambiguous and fascinating moral presence of the Agency in our national life for the last four decades," and thus he did not have to know someone personally or be in the agency to derive "the tone of its inner workings" (1169). In fact, he goes so far as to claim that his "imaginative CIA is as real or more real than nearly all of the lived-in ones" (1171). While many might debate such a point, his comment reflects his characteristic tendency to blur the lines between fact and fiction—and to demonstrate the ways in which those lines are always, already, inevitably blurred in life itself. This is particularly evident when he attempts to inhabit the minds of historical figures, as he does in *Harlot's Ghost*. Some of these figures, such as Fidel Castro, JKF, and Mafia don Sam Giancana, appear only on the periphery of the narrative, and their representations are drawn primarily from documented fact, while fictionalized versions of real CIA operatives such as William King Harvey and E. Howard Hunt play a more central role. The concurrent existence of the real and imaginative constitutes just one kind of duality explored throughout the book.

Though *Harlot's Ghost* is a result of Mailer's abiding interest in the work of the CIA, the achievement of the novel is that it ultimately upends rather than supports the romanticization of the agency. As Mailer stated in an interview after the novel's release, "I thought it was worth doing a book in great detail about how these people worked because you know it's always fun to do a novel when you essentially respect the people you're writing about, but they're engaged in the wrong activity."[21] Throughout, Mailer draws attention to this "wrong activity" by pointing to the chaos within and the failures of the CIA, emphasizing that, much of the time, the members of the agency themselves know very little of what they are investigating. They are forced instead to focus their attention on mundane tasks with little to no concept of a larger project that allegedly works toward American national security. For example, Harry Hubbard's first assignment after formally joining the CIA quickly becomes a farce that invokes the satirical absurdity of a work like Joseph Heller's *Catch-22*. In this early stage of his career, Harry's inability to locate information on a particular CIA operative threatens to get him into trouble, so with the help of his godfather and mentor Hugh "Harlot" Montague, he changes his own code name in order to avoid demotion or reprimand. As a result, he is instructed to find out the identity of the unknown low-level clerk who could not find the original information; in other words, he ends up tasked with reporting on himself.

Mailer is also critical of the organization's leadership, emphasizing that even those in positions of power had little concept of the details of their respective missions, for much of the covert information under investigation is stalled, interrupted, or mistaken at all levels of command. In this way, *Harlot's Ghost* echoes *The Naked and the Dead,* wherein Mailer depicts American military officers to be as vulnerable and confused as many of their enlisted men. Moreover, like that first novel, *Harlot's Ghost* points to the moral corruption within upper levels of such a powerful organization. Mailer's epigraph to the novel, drawn from the Old Testament, foreshadows this theme:

> For we wrestle, not against flesh and blood,
> but against principalities, against powers,
> against the rulers of the darkness
> of this world, against spiritual wickedness
> in high places. (Ephesians 6:12)

Those individuals who become mired in bureaucracy, drunk with power, or slaves to the institution are in *Harlot's Ghost* most likely to be those who exemplify the "spiritual wickedness" in high places. As a result of the corruption, the miscommunication, the violence, the competition, the bureaucracy, and the masculine posturing he witnesses and experiences, Harry determines early on that "insanity did not exist across the sea from reality, but could be visited on foot" (199–200).

In addition to serving as a fictionalized investigation of the CIA, *Harlot's Ghost* is at its core a bildungsroman about Harry Hubbard's coming of age; Hubbard himself, in fact, refers to his tale as such (97). Part of his journey towards manhood involves a dangerous climb, the familiar test of manhood that Mailer and his literary characters often undergo to test their existential masculine courage. Hugh "Harlot" Montague, Harry's godfather and mentor, encourages Harry to learn how to climb, and accompanies him on each trip. During these climbs, Harry learns that "happiness is experienced most directly in the intervals between terror" and that fear "has to be conquered or it invades one's dreams" (138). Though these tests of courage afford him respect from Harlot, from his family, and from himself, he struggles with other physical trials of masculinity that Mailer puts in front of many of his protagonists. For instance, Harry has trouble learning to fight; while boxing is part of his CIA training, he is unable to shake the memory of how he had faltered when confronted with a challenge as a young boy. As he reflects: "I thought a good deal . . . of the cousin who had knocked me down when he was eleven and I was nine, and how I had not risen to fight him back but merely watched blood fall from my nose to splash down on the ground, and with each drop, wished for it to be his blood. Now in the gym, when I worked on the heavy bag, something of that vast and near to long-lost rage came back to me" (187).

This is distressing to Harry, for much like his climbing efforts with Harlot, boxing is in this context a highly masculine sport that offers him the ability to "earn" his manhood. "In prison they say you have nothing but the standing achieved by your courage to stand up to other people," he says. "Courage may be your only capital, but that buys all the nutrients you need for your ego. I admire the simplicity, and the strength it takes to be that free a man" (958). At times, the masculine code to which Harry believes he must adhere extends into violence, albeit in his own life this violence remains latent. Prior to embarking on his mission to Cuba in the 1960s, he says (reminiscent of Rojack and Madden) that he "felt much impressed (and surprised) by the weight of the readiness of murder that sat in me" (662).

Still, true to form, Mailer does not imbue his protagonist with such an investment in masculine ideology unquestioningly. He also fashions in Harry an awareness of the faults embedded in the drive to earn one's masculinity through dangerous tests of physical and mental courage; he acknowledges that such feats are, at their core, attempts to avoid confronting vulnerabilities. As Harry recognizes, "Highly developed skills of evasion went into keeping ourselves removed from the center of our cowardice" (960). Moreover, it is not insignificant that Harlot—the model of masculine strength and confidence throughout the novel, and Harry's rival for the affections of Kittredge—is paralyzed after a failed climb later in his life. Thus, the very thing that afforded him a sense of his masculine power is also what ultimately emasculates him; additionally, after his accident (which, tragically, also kills his son), Kittredge leaves him.

Mailer extends this interrogation of masculinity to his construction of Harry's sexual desires—though here too, as he did in *Ancient Evenings,* he explores the *anxiety* created over so-called nonnormative desire, rather than the *embrace* of such. This is particularly evident in Harry's sexually fueled, ongoing rivalry with fellow CIA operative Dix Butler. "It irked me not to be able to enter the lists against him on the field of female conquest," Harry says, thus engaging in another brand of culturally endorsed masculine "testing" (256). Yet the sexual attraction between the two men is also undeniable, with Dix's advances marked as the more aggressive. "There's two kinds of sexual behavior between men," Dix says, "compulsion and mutual regard. The second does not exist until the first is attempted" (292). And later: "What if I were to push your face into the carpet, and manhandle your cherry pants off your cherry ass? Do you think I'm strong enough?" he asks Harry during one particularly heated exchange (291). Though he ultimately rejects Dix's advances, when initially contemplating whether to engage in such an encounter, Harry thinks, "I could steal something of his strength"—a comment similar to that made by Menenhetet in relation to Ramses II in *Ancient Evenings.*

Mailer continues to circle back to Harry's desires throughout the novel, showing Harry to be unsure what the embrace of such desire would do to his sense of self and his sense of masculinity.[22] For instance, later, when finding himself attracted to a transvestite named Libertad, Harry convinces himself that he is "not homosexual, but devoted to beauty, the beauty of women," since Libertad "has managed to absorb the quintessence of femininity" (608). Throughout this exploration of Harry's sexuality, it appears as though Mailer himself is still working to flesh out "the edges of the rich theme of homosexuality" (as Mailer put it in his 1955 essay "The Homosexual Villain") and still struggling to find a place for it in his construction of contemporary masculinity.[23]

Also significant to the theme of masculinity and sexuality in *Harlot's Ghost* is that part of Harry's affinity for Dix lies in their mutual experience of sexual abuse—Harry at the hands of a teacher, Dix at the hands of his brother. While Harry's experience leaves him wary of sex and relatively timid in general, Dix is more aggressive, more violent, and more open about the way he fought his abuse. This is perhaps why Harry finds him so magnetizing—he is a model of a different kind of masculinity. As Marina Rosenthal aptly points out, this also makes Dix particularly fitting for the CIA in ways that Harry perhaps is not: "In Mailer's eyes, the CIA demands a squad of agents who are impervious to painful experiences and are even able to capitalize on their trauma. Doing so, they generate more effective aggression to fill the agency's need for spies who are willing to secure intelligence in any way necessary."[24]

Primarily, though, Harry's desire is directed toward Kittredge Montague, Harlot's wife. Throughout the novel, Harry and Kittredge exchange a series of letters, which reflect the ebb and flow of their attraction and emotional connection—though it is not until many years after the novel's central events that they eventually consummate their relationship. While Kittredge is not a fully developed female character (this novel, like many of Mailer's works, is staunchly male-centered), neither is she merely poised as a peripheral love interest. Rather, Mailer uses Kittredge to ventriloquize his own philosophy of duality and his longstanding interest in the opposing forces of the human psyche—specifically, those he posits to be dictated by gender. Kittredge, for example, has penned a detailed thesis regarding concepts of "Alpha" and

"Omega"—opposites coexisting, with Omega "a little more responsive to nocturnal impulses than Alpha" and more "inclined to pessimism" (157). Alpha is descended from sperm, according to Kittredge, and Omega is from the ovum—they comprise male and female psyches. "The war between God and the Devil usually goes on in both psychic entities," she says, clearly espousing Mailer's own oft-cited beliefs. "Schizophrenics tend to separate good and evil altogether, but in more balanced people, God and the Devil fight not only in Alpha, but in Omega as well" (157). These dualities are meant to convey the "complexities of human personality"—something that Mailer explores in the book as well, in terms of sexuality, desire, morality, and truth (452).

Though Harry "resolves" the sexual tension with Kittredge when they marry after Harlot's death, that is the only resolution the book offers. In fact, the novel ends with the words "TO BE CONTINUED" (though Mailer never makes good on that promise). Even Harlot's death is not a certainty: in fact, when we leave Harry, he is evading not just the CIA at large, but Harlot himself, who he believes may be alive and bent on killing Harry. This is in keeping with the increasing paranoia Harry experiences throughout the book, perhaps an inevitable consequence of his involvement in the intrigues and deceits of the CIA. In fact, Harry (like Mailer himself) becomes fixated on possible conspiracies behind the deaths of JFK and Marilyn Monroe, particularly after being involved with a woman named Modene Murphy, who (in the novel's fictional constructs) may have been involved with JFK immediately prior to his death.

David Anshen has argued that the lack of resolution in the novel is a "valuable strategy in Mailer's efforts to present unpleasant realities of American society." The "gaps in knowledge," says Anshen, "present a consistent picture of inherent, systematic obstacles to effective activity."[25] Though the lack of a sequel was not so premeditated as Anshen's reading would suggest (Mailer did intend to continue the narrative, but was prevented by other projects), this remains an intriguing interpretation of the conclusion to *Harlot's Ghost*. It becomes especially useful in light of the novel's fixation on the unknowability of the human psyche—Kittredge's theory about human psychology, for instance, primarily proves that the individual is in a constant state of flux and internal struggle. Rather than providing any pat, fictionalized answers to the mysteries explored in the novel, Mailer chooses instead to pause in the space of uncertainty at the end—less satisfying, perhaps, in a work of fiction, but certainly more reflective of the "unpleasant realities of American society," which are after all what Mailer has proven to be so adept at exploring over the course of his career. Six years after *Harlot's Ghost,* in his brief novel *The Gospel According to the Son,* Mailer turns his attention to one of the dominant spiritual, historical, and mythical mysteries of Western culture and philosophy—and particularly, American culture in the twentieth century—the life of Jesus Christ.

Over the years, *The Gospel According to the Son* has been interpreted in a number of ways: it has been alternately deemed a manifestation of Mailer's existential philosophy, an example of his Manichaean or Gnostic beliefs, a controversial revision of Christian doctrine, and a novel about the age-old struggles between father and son.[26] The novel represents another chapter in Mailer's career-long fascination with paradox and dialectic, and here Mailer creates not only what some have identified as an embattled, "existential" Jesus, but also a more expansive embodiment of the kind of dialectic that defines so much of Mailer's work. Jesus's dual divinity and humanity comprise the most obvious of his paradoxical qualities, but also included are traits that might define any number of Mailer's characters who seem defined by unresolvable contradictions. Mailer's Jesus is vain and humble, self-assured and self-doubting, an advocate of peace who also embraces "the sword."

From his fashioning of Stephen Rojack in *An American Dream* to Gary Gilmore in *The Executioner's Song* to Harry Hubbard in *Harlot's Ghost,* Mailer has addressed moral and ethical complexities of life that often give rise to seeming contradictions. It may be no surprise, therefore, that Mailer would choose Jesus as a subject, for who better to represent this dialectic than one of the most embattled figures in religious lore? More than just a continuation of Mailer's earlier work, however, this characterization of Jesus allows Mailer to explore even more deeply the tension and interaction between opposing forces. In essence, Mailer's Jesus stands in the center of these dualities, a point around which they revolve and through which they are refracted. He not only creates an "existential" Jesus who searches for the meaning of his role on earth, and not just a Manichean figure caught in the midst of a battle between God and the devil, but also one who is riven by a contradiction that stems from four central and often paradoxical relationships that make up the content and structure of the narrative: truth and fiction, myth and history, good and evil, and humanity and divinity.

From the very beginning of the novel, Mailer relishes the complexity of his subject and its invitation for controversy by emphasizing the simultaneous truth and fiction of the Gospels. Mailer's Jesus in some ways tells us what we already know—that the Gospels themselves are a necessary blend of history and historical fiction. Of the Sermon on the Mount, for instance, he says: "They had me saying all manner of things, and some were the opposite of others. Matthew put so many sayings together, indeed, that he might as well have had me not ceasing to speak for a day and a night, and speaking out of two mouths that did not listen to each other" (111). He also informs us that while Matthew's gospel "would also claim that the wise men brought gifts of gold and frankincense and myrrh . . . that may not be true. For Joseph and Mary never spoke of such presents" (18). This focus on the blurring of truth and fiction in the Gospels prepares the reader for the narrative voice that structures the entire novel; essentially, it allows Mailer to fashion a narrator who knows more than we do, and more than the Jesus represented in the Gospels—for here Jesus returns and offers commentary. It is a postmodern, metafictional Jesus in many ways, a Jesus who comments on the representation of himself, drawing attention to the constructed nature of his legend.

This commentary is also Mailer's way of criticizing the license taken by the Christian church, particularly its use of the Gospels for individual financial gain that has led to factions within the church itself. Of the Gospel writers, Mailer's Jesus says: "Since each looked to give strength to his own church, how could he not fail to mix what was true into all that was not?" He also notes, however, that "from all these churches one prevailed, and it chose but four gospels, condemning the others for placing 'immaculate and sacred words' next to 'shameless lies'" (4). The problem, then, is not necessarily the blending of truth and fiction, but the Christian church's veneration of these Gospels as sacred truths and nothing else. While critical of this, Mailer maintains a sense of humor as he exposes these problems, and there is a subtle wink behind some of his Jesus's statements about truth. "This is the truth of why we took that journey," he says of Joseph and Mary's journey from Nazareth to Bethlehem, "and it is also true that I was born in a manger by the light of a candle. As we all know by now, there was no room at the inn" (15). By having his Jesus assert what is true directly after he pointed us to the near impossibility of discerning truth from fiction in the Gospels, Mailer draws us into the game, implicating us in his own questioning of whether we can decipher what is history and what is fabrication, and his exploration of how those two phenomena can exist together in the Gospels themselves.

This focus on the simultaneous existence of historical fiction and hearsay, and on how oral tradition passed down over thousands of years may have distorted what once was fact, also provides an outlet for Mailer to engage with the more puzzling, mythical aspects of the Gospels. As he explores the blurred lines between myth and history that define the Gospels, Mailer both embraces and critiques the magic and mysticism that surround Christianity's definition of Jesus. In a certain sense the novel takes the narratives of Jesus's miracles for granted—Jesus as narrator admits that he did, in fact, turn water into wine and multiply the loaves and the fishes—but the circumstances surrounding these miracles are revised to better fit a characterization of Jesus who is himself more questioning, more conflicted, and perhaps more human than the one depicted in the Gospels. We are asked to suspend our disbelief, perhaps, in light of Jesus's matter-of fact- appraisal of the element of magic in carpentry. "A fine piece worked upon for days might betray your tool at the smallest mistake, and often the board seemed to split by itself," he says. "I came to believe that even a crude plank could act with knowledge of good and evil (and much desire to do the latter)" (6). At the same time, Mailer's Jesus also calls into question what has become a largely unquestioned belief in his ability to perform miracles. "Exaggeration is the language of the Devil," he says, after explaining how the Gospels inflated the story of the loaves and the fishes. He corrects our understanding of this miracle, noting, "When each person had tasted these fragments, so do I believe that each morsel became enlarged within his thoughts. . . . This was a triumph of the Spirit rather than an enlargement of matter" (116).

Jesus's simultaneous encompassing of both good and evil is another central aspect of Mailer's examination of paradox. On the surface, we might recognize this duality as simply another aspect of Jesus's humanity. After all, Mailer had already been discussing the concepts of good and evil throughout his career, and they are made manifest in many of his conflicted human characters. Yet here Mailer seems to take this discussion to a new level, foreshadowing his even more ambitious exploration of these themes in his 2007 novel, *The Castle in the Forest*. There is a certain boldness to Mailer's expanded discussion of Jesus's human weakness in the face of temptation, for it is represented not merely as a test that Jesus eventually "passes" but something that plagues him for the remainder of the novel, such that what we might call simple "human weakness" often takes the upper hand over his divine inclinations. For instance, after the temptation in the desert, Mailer's Jesus continues to wonder whether he's chosen the right side. Employing language reminiscent of Stephen Rojack in *An American Dream*, Jesus admits he is puzzled because the devil "did not inspire fear but comfort," and that though "his odor could leave me uneasy, it also offered sympathy to desires I had not yet allowed myself to feel" (48). Even as he refuses the temptation in the desert, saying to he devil, "It is not you I want. It is my father," he admits, "Even as I said this, I knew a small but sharp woe. I was losing something I desired, and I was losing it forever" (56).

This conflict between good and evil is also embodied in Jesus's language, wherein he feels not only torn between these forces, but also rendered more powerful by embodying both of them. Riding the horse into Jerusalem, Jesus claims he "felt like the master of good and evil" (150). He refers to himself as speaking with a "forked tongue" and admits: "I had said it was easier tor a camel to pass through the eye of a needle than for a rich man to enter the

Kingdom of Heaven, yet from the other side of my mouth, I had, if only for an instant, been scornful of the poor" (194). These almost manipulative gifts as a speaker, as he claims to believe, are derived from a combination of both God and Satan; as he says, "I could feel how God had enabled me to steal a few skills from the Devil. In truth, I could now employ Satan's manner when speaking. I would address strangers with the finest courtesy and the most intimate exhilaration, as if we shared among ourselves the wonder of many things unsaid" (68).

The language of the novel has been a point of mild controversy not because of comments like these, but because some have criticized Mailer's book for its lack of inventiveness, claiming that it leans too heavily on the text of the Gospels themselves. Michiko Kakutani, for instance, has argued that everything in the book is "a pale, user-friendly version of what it is in the Bible." She seems simultaneously distressed over the ways in which the novel does *not* resemble the Bible, claiming Mailer's Jesus sounds like "a chatty cult leader," "a guest on Oprah," and "Luke Skywalker" and that his language is alternately sarcastic, boastful, and complaining.[27] However, this act of borrowing is, in many ways, the stylistic "point" of the novel: Mailer makes deliberate choices about which quotes he selects from the Gospels and how he chooses to weave them in with his own prose, with the overall effect of depicting a being who is, in his own words, "half a man and half something else, something larger." This combination of the verbatim quotes from the Bible and the complaining, prideful, or conflicted language that Mailer also attributes to this figure allows him to further probe the supposed divisions between good and evil, human and divine, and to explore the nuances and contradictions of this mytho-historical figure.

For instance, if we take a closer look at the quotes he chose specifically to help draw his figure of Jesus, we can see that these too speak directly to this fixation on paradox. These carefully selected quotes demonstrate the contradictions embedded within the language of the Gospels themselves, particularly Jesus's rhetorically paradoxical advice: variations on "If any of you is filled with the desire to be first, know that he shall be last," for example, is quoted twice (129). The inclusion of these quotes, coupled with the language and interior monologue that Mailer attributes to his fictional Jesus, points to his deeper examination of the problems inherent in the language of the Bible. Moreover, the language also invites readers to see the ways in which notions of truth and fiction, good and evil, myth and history, are slippery and indefinable terms—though much of Christian doctrine might have us believe otherwise.

Finally, Mailer explores the conflict introduced by a figure of Jesus whose goal is supposedly to bring peace, but who does so by first bringing violence. "'I have not come to send peace but a sword,'" he says—a quote not of Mailer's own making, but taken directly from the Gospel of Matthew. (This is similar to a line from Luke's Gospel: "if you don't have a sword, sell your cloak and buy one.") This is often seen to be one of the more controversial statements attributed to the figure of Jesus in the Bible, and one that flies in the face of his peace-driven mission. It suggests, of course, that Jesus embraced certain kinds of violence, in the name of certain kinds of justice—qualifications that Mailer himself has also made throughout his fiction, as he has often included some variation on the idea that violence has creative potential. (In "The White Negro" he offered the idea that certain kinds of violence can lead to "violence's opposite," for instance, but in a 1962 interview, he also emphasized that what he disapproves of is "*inhuman* violence—violence which is on a large scale and abstract.")

In light of this distinction, the vision of "many battles" anticipated by Mailer's Jesus speaks to the kind of existential violence that is a familiar focus of much of Mailer's fiction—one that contains within it a redeeming power. And thus, as with his careful selection of quotes from the Gospels, Mailer is not imposing but merely *finding* contradiction in the already existent representation of Jesus, a figure whose entire mission of peace in Christian doctrine is founded on one singular act of extreme violence—albeit one that he suffers rather than deploys. Yet beyond this, Mailer is able to embellish the contradiction, crafting a version of Jesus who not only seeks peace through violence to explain this need for an "army of apostles," but also claims to draw from the language of Pontius Pilate to explain his motives. "I must remember Pontius Pilate, who said that in peace there was no truth, and in truth, no peace," says Mailer's Jesus, thus undermining any attempts to understand his tale as one of simple binaries—allowing Mailer to fashion a strange loop in which violence brings peace and peace seems to preclude truth.

In an interview with Charlie Rose, Mailer notes that, from the very beginning, his goal was to write about Jesus "as a man" but also "to make a novel out of the central myth or keel of Western civilization." This explanation of Jesus as not just human and divine but also mythical points in many ways to the impossibility of concretely defining a character who embodies such fundamentally different characteristics. Thus, in a final twist, a novel that would seem to define the life of Jesus in fact points to the very indefinability of such a figure. Mailer continued to demonstrate his fascination with such unknowable figures—those who seem to defy relatability and conclusive interpretation, who embody contradiction and duality—until the end of his career; indeed, it is the focus of his final novel, 2007's *The Castle in the Forest.*

CHAPTER 7

Concluding with Questions

In the work he published during the last decade of his life, Mailer continued to expound on the ideas and philosophies that had intrigued him throughout his career. In later essays and interviews, including those published in *The Big Empty* (2006) and *On God* (2007), Mailer offers some of his sharpest and most poignant cultural commentaries, sustaining his critical appraisal of the American political system and the country's political leaders. In *Why Are We At War?* (2003), Mailer scrutinizes the George W. Bush administration's decision to deploy American troops to Iraq, questioning the administration's motives and arguing that the decision had less to do with American safety and more to do with the myth of an American empire. Though Mailer says Bush is the "immediate obstacle" to American democracy and a "collection of disasters" (for "what he does to the English language is a species of catastrophe all by itself"), no one escapes his incisive analysis, as he refuses to side with any one political party while the left and right become increasingly polarized in twenty-first-century America. For example, in *The Big Empty,* he critiques both George W. Bush and John Kerry during the run-up to the 2004 presidential election, predicting that Kerry, if elected, "will go along too much with the corporations who . . . are running America" (24). More than any single politician, Mailer is most concerned about the political system at large, which forces individual politicians to submit to corporate power, of which Mailer remains unfailingly skeptical. Ultimately, Mailer believes, American politicians are "working against forces greater than themselves" (24).

Mailer also weighs in on the conversation surrounding patriotism and American exceptionalism, ideas that gained strength after 9/11. In *The Big Empty,* for instance, he argues that the Bush administration is made up of "the tycoons of the oil industry, plus neoconservatives, plus gung-ho militarists," three different groups that are united in their belief in American exceptionalism. "They believe God wanted America to rule the world," Mailer says. "All too many Americans do believe that. Just look at the patriotic fever every time there's an occasion for people to show their flags. Very few fascist nations ever failed to put a huge emphasis on getting people to wave flags. This is not the same as calling America fascistic . . . but . . . I would say America could be approaching a pre-fascistic condition" (39). Such commentary recalls Mailer's qualms about the climate of post–World War II America, expressed decades earlier in *The Naked and the Dead* by General Cummings, who believes America is going to "absorb" the dream of fascism that Germany attempted to execute because "when you've created power, materials, armies, they don't wither of their own accord" (321).

Part of Mailer's fear of patriotism is that, in his mind, it dulls the intelligence and critical thinking faculties of the average American. As he would say in 2006: "Democracy depends on the intelligence of the people. By that, I don't mean literary intelligence or even verbal intelligence. Rather, it is a readiness to look into the face of difficult questions and not search for quick answers. You can measure real intelligence by that ability to live with a difficult question. And patriotism gobbled up, sentimentalized, and thereby abased is one of the most powerful single forces to proliferate stupidity."[1] Of course, Mailer did remain concerned with the life of "literary intelligence." In a 1998 interview with Sean Abbott, Mailer laments, "Literature . . . has been ground down in the 20th century"; he predicts that soon "the profound novel will be a curiosity."[2] Indeed, the place of literature in the United States has certainly shifted and waned in recent decades, making Mailer's comments all the more prescient.

Mailer himself, however, contributed to the life of the novel until his death. His final work of fiction, *The Castle in the Forest* (2007), exhibits his lasting devotion to asking life's large, existential, spiritual questions while continuing to examine dualities and attempting to explore the psyche of history's most controversial figures. This novel in particular focuses on the ancestry and early life of Adolf Hitler, imagining his childhood and the various circumstances that may have contributed to his infamous deeds as an adult. The tale is narrated by a devil named Dieter, or "D.T." for short, who in the structure of Mailer's conception of hell holds a position equivalent to middle management, and who finds himself laden with the responsibility of observing the young Adolf. D.T. narrates the tale retrospectively, thus sharing the historical knowledge of the modern reader, and very much aware of the ongoing fascination with the figure of Adolf Hitler in contemporary society. "Even today," he says, "the first obsession remains Hitler. Where is the German who does not try to understand him? Yet where can you find one who is content with the answer?" (9). D.T.

goes on to add that, despite this fixation, the mystery surrounding Hitler has led to an "impoverished understanding" of his personality. He also, however, assures the reader that he, in contrast to most, can "comprehend [the] psyche" of Hitler (72), that in fact he knows him "top to bottom" and "from asshole to appetite" (9).

By making D.T. the narrator of his tale, Mailer also introduces another form of narrative perspective: an omniscient first-person narrator who is also a character in the tale, and who thus allows Mailer to avoid the limitations of a "curious" and "unnatural" traditional first-person perspective, as he once put it, as well as the limitations of his third-person personal perspective. With his narrator, Mailer also sets up quite an ambitious and certainly controversial project for himself, since as author and creator of D.T.'s perspective, he is also the literary architect behind this insight into the psyche of Hitler. This in turn suggests that over the course of the five hundred pages in which this hitherto mysterious psyche is explored, we as readers, being privy to someone else's understanding of Hitler's childhood and character, might also be asked to develop some kind of empathy for him, a concept that can be quite difficult to absorb.

Yet as it turns out, the real controversy and achievement of the novel lie not so much in what it reveals of the mind of Adolf Hitler—since in truth we get very little of that here, aside from some of his childhood thoughts and musings—but in what it reveals about humanity's longstanding moral questions. Specifically, the novel embodies a central problem or question often encountered when talking about evil in general: should it be framed as something exceptional or something banal? Mailer himself grappled with this question throughout much of his career, incorporating into many of his works ruminations on an ongoing existential battle between God and Satan, and reflecting on what that battle might suggest about the nature of evil. Recall, for instance, his remarks in *The Presidential Papers,* where he refers to an existential God who discovers both "the possibilities and limitations of his creative powers," and an "existential equal to God, an antagonist, the Devil, a principle of Evil whose signature was the concentration camps, whose joy is to waste substance, whose intent is to prevent God's conception of being from reaching its mysterious goal" (193). Here Mailer pits good against evil, but attributes equal amounts of power to both, suggesting the notion of a limited and imperfect God, whose power is not, in fact, so distant or different from that of the devil, and whose image is reflected in the triumphs *and* failures of human existence. In this way, both forces might even be seen as unexceptional in their imperfection. At the same time, Mailer clearly suggests that, if good and evil are not exceptional in and of themselves, there are, perhaps, exceptional *kinds* of good and evil. If some "mysterious goal" is the epitome of God's goodness, then the "signature" of the Holocaust is the nadir of Satan's evil.

Thus, *The Castle in the Forest* also invites readers to ask: where does the more familiar battle of good and evil that is, in Mailer's view, present everywhere around us, leave off—and how do we define what makes something—or someone, like Hitler—singularly evil? As Mailer crafts an origin story for one of history's perhaps most unknowable figures, he paradoxically mythicizes and humanizes Hitler, simultaneously placing Hitler on a level separate from the rest of humanity while also fashioning him into a victim of circumstance or a mere pawn of the devil. That is, while Mailer represents evil as a corrupted good in Hitler's adolescence, occasioned by circumstance and even banal, he also repeatedly emphasizes the ways in which everything about Hitler's early life is unique, from his conception to the close attention he receives at a young age from Satan himself. The implications of both of these definitions are problematic: to suggest that evil is commonplace, particularly in the case of a figure like Hitler, is to open oneself up to criticisms similar to those Hannah Arendt faced upon her publication of *Eichmann in Jerusalem*. Arendt reflected on what she called the "banality of evil" exhibited by Nazi soldiers, particularly Eichmann, a man whose trial sparked a very public discussion of evil, but who exhibited no remarkable qualities or psychopathic behaviors, and merely claimed to be following orders. Critics of her thesis argued that associating crimes of the Holocaust with the mundane or the banal threatened to take some accountability away from the accused. Yet to assign evil an extraordinary status is to, in effect, place it on a pedestal, out of reach, where we are unable to understand or combat its serious implications. Mailer himself seemed to recognize this dilemma, as he constantly seems to question his own representation of such evil in the text.

For instance, from the very start of the novel, as though to undermine or overturn any assumptions readers might have about the strange or extraordinary nature of Adolf Hitler's personality, Mailer has D.T. continually emphasize that there was nothing special about Hitler; this is also reinforced by his referring to Hitler throughout the novel by the more benign and less historically encumbered name of Adi. As he envisions Hitler's childhood, Mailer, via D.T., suggests that his actions in adulthood might be attributed to a number of more commonplace or predictable psychological factors: his father abuses him, his mother over-loves him and then ignores him when a new son is born, his siblings mistreat him, his confidence is low, and he is tangentially, though not decidedly, responsible for the death of his younger brother Edmund—for which he feels pain and guilt, but a pain that is overshadowed by his growing resentment toward his parents for what he sees to be their clear favoritism of Edmund even after death. All of this, D.T. informs us, leads to a kind of "ineradicable melancholia" that seems to only increase throughout the years of young Adolf's childhood (330).

In these various explanations for the origins of Hitler's later actions, Mailer depicts evil in the novel as what Jeffrey Partridge has described as a "perversion of good."[3] Klara Hitler's excessive mothering of her son, for instance, is delivered with only the best of intentions—but becomes an example, perhaps, of "too much of a good thing." As D.T. tells us, Klara loves Adolf "past any measure of large maternal love," which Satan and his devils find "useful" since they "are keyed to look for excess of every kind, good or bad, loving or hateful" (74). That evil might be considered here as some form of good gone awry does not make it trivial, but it does indicate that the average person might understand it in some way—after all, this notion of evil arises from relatable and familiar actions and emotions, simply and unfortunately offered in excess. In Mailer's vision, Hitler seems primed to resemble something akin to Denise Levertov's profile of Eichmann as "a pitiful man whom none / pity, whom all / must pity if they look / into their own face."[4]

However, other moments belie both suggestions that Hitler's childhood is nothing very special, and that the circumstances in his life are merely a perverted good. While D.T. repeatedly responds to events in Adi's childhood by dismissing their significance, these events are too purposefully—and at times, humorously—connected to what readers know will occur in his future to be purely coincidental or insignificant. For example, Mailer recounts young Adolf's fascination with the gassing of the "contaminated" bees in his father's hive, which inspires simultaneous horror and glee. He notes that the school he attends—the place where he begins to develop his powers as an orator even at a young age—has a swastika over the gate. And when Adolf masturbates, he would "practice holding his arm in the air at a forty-five-degree angle for a long time" (457).

D.T. also makes a point on several occasions of attesting to ways that evil has been selectively and deliberately placed into Hitler's life. D.T. himself acknowledges that he has "spoken at . . . length of our cautious process of selection because I wish to emphasize how uncommon was the special attention given to Adi for his early years" (110). He also adds, "The odds were that he would creep through life with a self-protective ego . . . if the Evil One had not been present at his conception" (111). What Mailer calls "dream etchings"—dreams planted or "etched" into Adi's mind—also factor into this representation of evil. As D.T. explains, "A direct communication from the Maestro had arrived—I was to implant a particular dream into the head of our six-year-old. *Etch* was the salient verb. 'I want you,' he said, 'to etch Adi's brain with a permanent notion'" (159). Through these dreams, D.T. makes Adi believe, for example, that "he would yet become God's gift to the people, fierce as fire, as strong as steel" (394). He also fortifies Adolf's "sense of the power that murder can offer the murderer" (399) and embeds in young Adolf's mind the idea that "blood possesses magic"—a likely allusion to Hitler's obsession with racial purification.

Taking these contradictions a step further, Mailer also makes young Adi's childhood so exceptional that even D.T. claims not to understand his actions. Once, for instance, Adi believes he can kill a mouse "by the force of his thoughts," an idea which D.T. insists he did not plant. "I knew the limitations of my agents," he says. "They could not have conceived of such a notion. This had come from Adi. It was his. His alone" (191). Adolf's excitement over the burning of the bees also seems to puzzle even D.T. In this way, Mailer has D.T. confer a heavier responsibility on Adi as an individual, rather than on some abstract notion of evil, suggesting that perhaps young Adolf is developing into something that even Satan—or at least, his mid-level devils—cannot understand.

Thus, despite some arguments that in this novel Mailer turns away from a dualistic notion of evil, the treatment of good and evil seems to remain divided; while some instances might suggest evil as a "perverted good," others reject such a notion.[5] While Mailer does not offer any concrete "answers" about the nature of evil, particularly as it relates to the character of Adolf Hitler, the novel forces us to ask difficult questions about a fairly abstract concept. Mailer himself reminds us of this in the final pages, in which D.T. offers some concluding reflections. "What enables devils to survive," he says, "is that we are wise enough to understand there are no answers—there are only questions" (467). The important thing, he notes, is that "good questions still vibrate with honor within."

This idea of asking important questions and being able to live with "difficult answers" was something in which Mailer strongly believed throughout his life, as only through this kind of intelligent critical thinking, inquiry, conversation, and debate could the American individual—and America at large—truly grow into better and more compassionate beings. As he would note in *On God*, "The point is that the purpose of life may be to find higher and better questions" (75), and thus he encourages his readers "to have the honor to live with confusion" (77). Though in his early life Mailer may have developed a reputation as a hot-headed or belligerent public figure, such an image does not reflect the ways in which he himself was able to live with this confusion and to seriously engage with competing perspectives on politics, spirituality, relationships, and art. “I’m right and I’m wrong so often that I have no interest in convincing others to think the way I do,” he said later in life. “I’m interested, rather, that we all get better at thinking.”[6]

NOTES

Chapter 1—Understanding Norman Mailer

1. This is also the epigraph to Mailer's 1955 novel, *The Deer Park.*

2. Mailer, *Oswald's Tale,* 515–16.

3. Lennon, *Norman Mailer: A Double Life,* 410, 418.

4. Ibid., 563.

5. Mailer, *The Spooky Art,* 101.

6. Michael Johnson, "Norman Mailer," 1971, in *Will the Real Norman Mailer Please Stand Up?* ed. Adams, 173.

7. Philip Roth, "Writing American Fiction," 1961, in *Reading Myself and Others* (N.Y.: Random House, 2001), 170–71.

8. Joan Didion was one of the few to argue that Mailer *had* in fact published his great novel. As she wrote in her review of 1979's *The Executioner's Song,* "In fact he has written this 'big book' at least three times now. He wrote it the first time in 1955 with 'The Deer Park' and he wrote it a second time in 1963 with 'An American Dream' and he wrote it a third time in 1967 with 'Why Are We in Vietnam?' and now, with 'The Executioner's Song,' he has probably written it a fourth" ("I Want to Go Ahead and Do It," *New York Times,* 7 October 1979).

9. "Norman Mailer: The Art of Fiction, No. 32," interview with Steven Marcus, *The Paris Review* 3 (1964), rpt. in *Conversations with Norman Mailer,* 85.

10. Mailer, Preface to *The Joker* (N.Y.: Warner, 1974), 15.

11. Lennon, *Norman Mailer: A Double Life,* 117.

12. W. J. Weatherby examines this relationship in detail in his 1977 book, *Squaring Off: Mailer vs. Baldwin* (N.Y.: Mason/Charter).

13. Schultz, *Buckley and Mailer,* 32.

14. Mailer, *Spooky Art,* 74.

15. "Mailer Opus," interview with Sean Abbott, *At Random Magazine,* May 1998, rpt. in Mailer, *Spooky Art,* 86.

16. Mailer, *Spooky Art,* 127. These remarks were first made in an interview with Michael Lennon, "An Author's Identity," published in *Pieces and Pontifications.*

17. Mailer, *The Presidential Papers* (N.Y.: Bantam Books, 1964), 194. All subsequent quotations are taken from this edition.

18. Mailer emphasized this central tenet of existentialism for most of his career. In a 1975 interview with Laura Adams, he similarly stated, "We find ourselves in an existential situation whenever we are in a situation where we cannot foretell the end" ("Existential Aesthetics: An Interview with Norman Mailer," *Conversations with Norman Mailer,* 213).

19. *On God,* 17.

20. Glenday, *Norman Mailer,* 5.

21. Nermeen Shaikh, "Interview with Norman Mailer," *Nextbook Reader* 4 (Spring 2007): 3.

22. *Selected Letters of Norman Mailer,* 519.

23. "Norman Mailer: The Art of Fiction, No. 32," interview with Steven Marcus, *The Paris Review,* Spring 1964, rpt. in *Conversations with Norman Mailer,* 89.

24. Mashey Bernstein, "The Mitzvot of Norman Mailer," *Jerusalem Post,* 14 November 2007. Web. 16 September 2015: http://www.jpost.com/Jewish-World/Jewish-Features/The-mitzvot-of-Norman-Mailer. For further analysis on this topic, also see Bernstein, "Jewish Values in the Fiction of Norman Mailer."

25. Mailer, *The Big Empty,* 126–27. This text is a collection of previously published excerpts and speeches, interspersed with transcribed conversations between Norman Mailer and his son, John Buffalo Mailer.

26. Mailer, *Advertisements for Myself* (N.Y.: Putnam's Berkeley Medallion, 1966), 46. All subsequent quotations are from this edition.

27. Mailer, *Pieces and Pontifications,* 28.

28. Mailer, *Presidential Papers,* 136.

29. Quoted in Barry Leeds, *The Enduring Vision of Norman Mailer,* 50.

30. Tony Tanner, *City of Words: American Fiction 1950–1970* (N.Y.: Harper & Row, 1971), 370.

31. "The Art of Fiction, No. 193," interview with Andrew O'Hagan, *The Paris Review* 181 (Summer 2007): https://www.theparisreview.org/interviews/5775/norman-mailer-the-art-of-fiction-no-193-norman-mailer.

32. Edmundson, "Romantic Self-Creations: Mailer and Gilmore in *The Executioner's Song,*" 434.

33. Whalen-Bridge, ed., *Norman Mailer's Later Fictions:* Ancient Evenings *through* Castle in the Forest, 189.

Chapter 2—*The Naked and the Dead* and Its Aftermath

1. Mailer, *Advertisements for Myself,* 85.

2. David Dempsey, "The Dusty Answer of Modern War," *New York Times,* 9 May 1948; Raymond Rosenthal, "Underside of the War," *Commentary,* 1 July 1948. The book was also adapted to film by Raoul Walsh but was critically panned, and Mailer hated it. When asked during a 1970 interview with Joseph Gelmis what he thought of the film, Mailer responded, "Considering what they could have had, I think it is the worst movie I've ever seen" (*Conversations with Norman Mailer,* 172).

3. Bufithis, "A Dialogue Essay on Mailer and Hemingway," *Mailer Review* 4 (2010): 69. Hemingway may not have appreciated this comparison. In his 1966 book *Papa Hemingway,* A. E. Hotchner cites Hemingway's less than favorable opinion of *The Naked and the Dead*: "The guy who wrote *The Naked and the Dead*—what's his name, Mailer—was in bad need of a manager. . . . The whole book's just diarrhea of the typewriter" (113). But at the same time, Gregory Hemingway notes that Ernest once called Mailer "probably the best postwar writer. . . . chances are he won't be able to throw another fit like *The Naked and the Dead*, but if he does . . . I better watch out" (*Papa: A Personal Memoir* [N.Y.: Houghton Mifflin, 1976], 103).

4. Vincent Casaregola, *Theaters of War: America's Perceptions of World War II* (N.Y.: Palgrave Macmillan, 2009), 168.

5. All subsequent quotes from the novel are taken from the Henry Holt & Co., 1998 edition.

6. This will be the first of several works in which Mailer subtly questions heteronormative masculinity. He will do this later most notably in *Ancient Evenings* (1983) and *Harlot's Ghost* (1991).

7. Leigh, *Radical Fictions and the Novels of Norman Mailer,* 20; Waldron, "The Naked, the Dead, and the Machine: A New Look at Norman Mailer's First Novel," *PMLA* 87, no. 2 (March 1972): 277.

8. *Conversations with Norman Mailer,* 14.

9. Cappell, "Hemingway's Jewish Progeny: Roth and Goldstein in *The Naked and the Dead,*" 209.

10. This racialization and feminization has been chronicled by such critics as Sander Gilman, Daniel Boyarin, Paul Breines, and Warren Rosenberg. As Neil Davison has argued in *Jewishness and Masculinity from the Modern to the Postmodern* (N.Y.: Routledge, 2010), perceptions of a "malignantly feminine" Jewish masculinity were reasserted throughout the nineteenth century by such renowned Jewish scholars and philosophers as Sigmund Freud, Otto Weininger, and Theodor Herzl, whose internalization of the concept of the "feminized Jew" led them to call for a "remasculinization" of Jewishness (26).

11. In an interview with Louise Levitas in 1948, Mailer said that what formed the book was "the feeling that people in our government were leading us into war again. The last half was written on this nerve right in the pit of my stomach" (*Conversations with Norman Mailer,* 4).

12. In *Ernest Hemingway, Men at War* (1942, NY: Bramball House, 1955, xi-xii), Hemingway also argued that America must be careful that "while we are fighting Fascism we do not slip into the ideas and ideals of Fascism."

13. Wilson, "Control and Freedom in *The Naked and the Dead,*" 164, 167.

14. Mailer, *The Big Empty,* 74.

15. Mailer, *Presidential Papers,* 136.

16. Many of Mailer's later works would also be criticized for "thin" or convoluted plots: *Tough Guys Don't Dance, Ancient Evenings,* and *Harlot's Ghost* are among these. Mailer later addressed the problem in *On God*. "The reason I don't like plots to prevail," Mailer says there, "is that they don't allow the figures in the book, the characters, to push their own limits to the point where they make the plot unacceptable and so push the design into chaos" (151).

17. Quotation from Mailer's acceptance speech for the National Book Foundation's Medal for Distinguished Contribution to American Letters, 16 November 2005.

18. Mailer, *Advertisements for Myself,* 87.

19. Norman Podhoretz, Preface to *Barbary Shore* (N.Y.: Grosset & Dunlap, 1963), xi. All subsequent quotes from the novel are taken from this edition.

20. Mailer, too, believed the Holocaust was a defining moment of the twentieth century and that it altered everything—perhaps even the process of karma and reincarnation, as he states in *On God*. However, unlike Lannie, he does not believe that good and evil ceased to exist as a result.

21. Anshen, "The Prescience of Mailer's Marxism: Socialism or Barbary Shore," 262.

22. Podhoretz, Preface to *Barbary Shore,* xii.

23. All quotations from Putnam's Berkeley Medallion edition (N.Y., 1967).

24. Bufithis, *Norman Mailer,* 51.

25. Such a comment anticipates Mailer's later remarks about acting and performance in 1967's "Some Dirt in the Talk" (rpt. in *Mailer Review* 3 [2009]: 447–48). In that piece, which covers the time he spent making his experimental film *Wild 90,* Mailer states that he himself is always acting—and that the average person is often a better actor than most professional actors.

26. Leeds, *The Structured Vision of Norman Mailer,* 113, 119.

27. Mailer, *Advertisements for Myself,* 212.

28. Ibid.

29. Ibid, 219.

30. Ibid, 211.

Chapter 3—An American Voice and *An American Dream*

1. Decter, "Mailer's Campaign,", 83–84.

2. Solotaroff, *Down Mailer's Way,* 139–40.

3. Mailer, *Advertisements for Myself,* 313.

4. The creative potential of violence was something Mailer believed in for most of his life. "If you cut all the violence out of society," Mailer told Lawrence Grobel in 2001, "you also cut out all the creativity" ("Norman Mailer: Stupidity Brings Out Violence in Me," *Mailer Review* 2 [Fall 2008]: 439, rpt. from Grobel, Lawrence. *Endangered Species: Writers Talk About Their Craft, Their Visions, Their Lives.* De Capo Press, 2001).

5. Mailer, *Advertisements for Myself,* 328.

6. Ibid., 292.

7. Ibid., 327.

8. Ibid., 313.

9. Ibid., 321.

10. Baldwin, "The Black Boy Looks at the White Boy," 270.

11. Ibid., 277.

12. Mailer, *Advertisements for Myself,* 288.

13. Ibid., 336.

14. Lennon, *Norman Mailer: A Double Life,* 220–21.

15. This idea is repeated almost verbatim in *Cannibals and Christians,* in which Mailer admits, "It has been the continuing obsession of this writer that the world is entering a time of plague. And the continuing metaphor for the obsession—a most disagreeable metaphor—has been cancer" (18).

16. Mailer, *Presidential Papers,* 22.

17. This harkens back to the ideas he espoused in "The White Negro," in which he advocated living a life of danger, on the margin—to practice a "hip" lifestyle which would "return us to ourselves."

18. Mailer, *Presidential Papers,* 134.

19. Recall his comment that Croft in *The Naked and the Dead* was a character for whom he held "secret admiration," largely because of his obsession with violence.

20. Kaufmann, *Norman Mailer: The Countdown,* 87.

21. Richard Slotkin investigates the way this mythology of the West has pervaded American history, culture, and literature in his influential trilogy of books, which include *Regeneration Through Violence* (1973), *The Fatal Environment* (1985), and *Gunfighter Nation* (1992).

22. "Norman Mailer Interviews Himself," *New York Times Review of Books,* 17 September 1967, 5; Didion, "A Social Eye," *National Review,* 20 April 1965, 329.

23. Frank McConnell, *Four Postwar Novelists: Bellow, Mailer, Barth and Pynchon* (Chicago: U of Chicago P, 1977), 96. Likewise, Michael Glenday says *An American Dream* "dramatized the national mood" (*Norman Mailer,* 88), for in the aftermath of Kennedy's assassination, "Americans were like cargo in the hold, loose and ready to slide, ready, like Rojack, to spill the blood of others" (93).

24. I will be referring to the 1965 publication of *An American Dream* in its novel form, as opposed to the serialized version. All quotations are from the Random House Vintage International edition, 1999.

25. In her 1965 review "A Nightmare by Norman Mailer," for example, Elizabeth Hardwick deems the novel a "literary disaster," calling it "morally foolish and intellectually empty" (in Lucid, ed., *Norman Mailer: The Man and His Work,* 145). Donald L. Kaufmann concluded that "Mailer's theory of authentic violence finds no way for American morality to come to terms with a 'new nervous system' of a murderer" (*Norman Mailer: The Countdown,* 96), and even Philip Bufithis, who ranked An American Dream among the finest American novels, argued that it "does not hold up well on the ethical level" (*Norman Mailer,* 74).

26. Mailer had heard Miles Davis play in Harlem in the 1950s and greatly admired his work; later he discovered that, before he had met her, his fourth wife, Beverly Bentley, had been in a relationship with Davis. See Lennon, *Norman Mailer: A Double Life,* 328.

27. Adams, *Existential Battles: The Growth of Norman Mailer,* 89.

28. Mailer, *Advertisements for Myself,* 313.

29. Ibid., 329.

30. Laura Adams has argued that Mailer's emphasis on the necessity of masculine courage is based on the assumption embodied by this episode: that "if one is victorious he extracts from his defeated opponent some of his force, which is then used to sustain and nurture his own life" (*Existential Battles,* 5).

31. Mailer, *Cannibals and Christians* (N.Y.: Pinnacle Books, 1981), 143. All quotations are from this edition.

32. Fuchs, *The Limits of Ferocity: Sexual Aggression and Modern Literary Rebellion,* 309.

33. "Living Like Heroes," interview with Richard Wollheim, *New Statesman,* 1961, rpt. in *Conversations with Norman Mailer,* 66.

34. Leeds, *Enduring Vision of Norman Mailer,* 42.

35. Batchelor, "Visions of the American Dream: F. Scott Fitzgerald, Bob Dylan, and Norman Mailer," 85.

Chapter 4—Mailer on War, Women, Politics, and Film

1. "Art of Fiction," *The Paris Review* 181 (2007).

2. All quotations from *The Armies of the Night* are from the Penguin Signet edition, 1968.

3. Mosser, "Genre Bending in *The Armies of the Night,*" 307.

4. As Barry Leeds also notes, "The most striking thing about Mailer as protagonist is a new sense of modesty and personal limitation" (*Structured Vision of Norman Mailer,* 250).

5. Jonathan D'Amore, *American Authorship and Autobiographical Narrative: Mailer, Wideman, and Eggers* (N.Y.: Palgrave Macmillan, 2012), 41.

6. *Selected Letters of Norman Mailer,* 370.

7. Fulgham, "The Wise Blood of Norman Mailer: An Interpretation and Defense of *Why Are We in Vietnam?*" 338, 341. Additionally, Fulgham notes that "Mailer implies and perhaps confesses that there is nothing civilized about violence. . . . as long as we justify our blood lust and hunger for sexual dominancy, we are not civilized men, but baboons and hyenas and wolves" (343).

8. Solotaroff, *Down Mailer's Way,* 180.

9. *Time* magazine called it "a wildly turgid monologhorrhea," for example ("Hot Damn," 8 September 1967). Even Mailer claimed he "hate[d] to add all that obscenity" but had to include it because it "is the only metaphor to express the situation that produces Vietnam" ("Anything Goes: Taboos in Twilight," *Newsweek*, 13 November 1967, 76).

10. "Norman Mailer's Cherry Pie," *New York Times,* 8 September 1967, 37.

11. As more than one critic has noted, John Cassavetes was an influence on Mailer's films. Mailer, however, once noted he never liked Cassavetes's work, calling it "false improvisation" (Chaiken, "Author, Auteur: A Conversation with Norman Mailer," 410).

12. Mailer, "A Course in Filmmaking," 1971, rpt. in *Mailer Review* 3 (Fall 2009): 482.

13. Chaiken, "Author, Auteur," 409.

14. "When Irish Eyes Are Smiling, It's Norman Mailer," interview with Vincent Canby, 1968, rpt. in *Conversations with Norman Mailer,* 141.

15. Ibid., 144.

16. "Mailer, McLuhan, and Muggeridge: On Obscenity," interview with Bob Fulford, 1968, rpt. in *Conversations with Norman Mailer,* 128.

17. Mailer, "Some Dirt in the Talk," 447–48.

18. Ibid., 448.

19. Ibid., 453.

20. Cohen, "Making Masculinity and Unmaking Jewishness: Norman Mailer's Voice in *Wild 90* and *Beyond the Law,*" 192–93.

21. Mailer, "Course in Filmmaking," 499.

22. Ibid., 503.

23. Ibid.

24. Ibid., 504.

25. Mailer, "Some Dirt in the Talk," 464.

26. "The Film Director as Superstar," interview with Joseph Gelmis, 1970, rpt. in *Conversations with Norman Mailer,* 155.

27. Mailer offers further commentary on Nixon and his Democratic opponent George McGovern during the 1972 presidential campaign in *St. George and the Godfather,* another feat of political reportage in which Mailer again refers to himself in the third person (this time as the journalist "Aquarius").

28. Leeds, *Enduring Vision of Norman Mailer,* 27.

29. Mailer, *Presidential Papers,* 131.

Chapter 5—Exploring American Mysteries

1. In 1976, Mailer also published *Genius and Lust,* a critical analysis of the work of Henry Miller. While not an interpretive biography in the same vein as his other works during this period, this particular work is another example of Mailer's ongoing interest in different aspects of life writing.

2. Glenday, "From Monroe to Picasso: Norman Mailer and the Life Study," 350.

3. Ibid., 352.

4. The book, a best seller that was released to a series of positive reviews, featured a collection of pictures of Marilyn taken by a number of notable photographers, including Eve Arnold, Milton Greene, George Barris, and Bert Stern. Larry Schiller had originally commissioned Mailer to provide a relatively brief textual accompaniment for the photographs, but Mailer's profound interest in the project led to his extended interpretive biography.

5. Schiller's reflections here are from the preface to the 2011 Taschen edition of *Marilyn,* which features a condensed version of Mailer's original text, edited by J. Michael Lennon and accompanied by a selection of Bert Stern's photographs of Monroe.

6. All subsequent quotes are from the 2012 edition reissued by Virgin Books (a Random House Group).

7. "King of the Hill," *Life*, 19 March 1971, 36.

8. Barry Leeds, "He Was a Fighter: Boxing in Norman Mailer's Life and Work," *Mailer Review* 2 (Fall 2008): 385.

9. Fried, "Mailer's Boxing Journalism," 222.

10. Joyce Carol Oates, *On Boxing* (Hopewell, N.J.: Ecco P, 1994), 8, 52.

11. Ibid., 54.

12. Mailer, *Presidential Papers,* 237.

13. Ibid., 245.

14. Ibid., 247.

15. As Mailer explains, the book is "directly based on interviews, documents, records of court proceedings, and other original material. . . . More than one hundred people were interviewed face to face, plus a good number talked to by telephone. The total, before count was lost, came to something like three hundred separate sessions, and they range in length from fifteen minutes to four hours" (*Executioner's Song,* 1051).

16. Joan Didion, "I Want to Go Ahead and Do It."

17. Christopher Ricks, "Mailer's Psychopath," *London Review of Books,* 16 March 1980, rpt. in *Mailer Review* 2 (Fall 2008): 486.

18. Edmundson, "Romantic Self-Creations," 441.

19. Mailer, *Cannibals and Christians,* 367.

20. *Selected Letters of Norman Mailer,* 511.

21. Jack Abbott, *In the Belly of the Beast* (N.Y.: Random House, 1981).

22. *Selected Letters of Norman Mailer,* 562.

23. Ibid., 572.

24. Olshaker, "The Crime of His Time," *Mailer Review* 3 (2009): 95.

25. Barrie Balter, "Individualism in *Oswald's Tale* and *Libra*," *Mailer Review* 3 (Fall 2009): 134.

26. Further indicating his interest in the art world, Mailer also provided the text that accompanied John Naar's photographs of street art in 1974's *The Faith of Graffiti.*

27. "Norman Mailer," interview with Charles Ruas, *Conversations with American Writers* (N.Y.: Random House, 1985), 18–36, rpt. in Mailer, *Spooky Art* 156.

28. Mailer told Pete Hamill in an interview that he felt that Picasso "had the same sort of restlessness in his mind that I have in mine" ("Kindred Spirits," *Art News,* November 1995, 213). In fact, J. Michael Lennon calls *Picasso* Mailer's "most autobiographical" book (*Norman Mailer: A Double Life,* 686).

29. *Selected Letters of Norman Mailer,* 673.

30. Michiko Kakutani, "Egos and Outlaws: Like Attracts Like," *New York Times,* 29 September 1995.

Chapter 6—The Divided Self across Genre

1. See Sharon Churcher, "Norman Mailer Dashes Off a Hit," *New York Magazine,* 10 October 1983, 17; also see Dearborn, *Mailer: A Biography,* 368.

2. Harold Bloom, "Norman in Egypt," *New York Review of Books* 30, no. 7 (28 April 1983).

3. "Twelfth Round: An Interview with Norman Mailer," with Robert Begiebing, 1983, rpt. in *Conversations with Norman Mailer,* 323, 326.

4. Robert Begiebing, "Norman Mailer: The Magician as Tragic Hero," *Mailer Review,* Fall 2009, 630, rpt. from Begiebing's *Toward a New Synthesis* (1989).

5. Boone, *The Homoerotics of Orientalism,* 219.

6. Ibid., 221.

7. This discussion harkens back to Mailer's discussion of the subject in *The Prisoner of Sex,* where he was also interested in the way anal sex is used to enforce hierarchies of power within the prison system, rather than the way homosexuality functions in the everyday world as a natural and consensual part of one's identity.

8. Benjamin DeMott, "Norman Mailer's Egyptian Novel," *New York Times,* 10 April 1983.

9. Anthony Burgess, *99 Novels: The Best in English since 1939* (N.Y.: Summit Books, 1984).

10. Ashton Howley, "Imperial Mailer: *Ancient Evenings*", in *Norman Mailer's Later Fictions,* 107.

11. Mailer, *Presidential Papers,* 286, 291.

12. Richard Poirier, *Times Literary Supplement,* 10 June 1983, 591–92.

13. Christopher Ricks, "Mailer's Primal Words," *Grand Street* 3 (Autumn 1983): 162.

14. James Emmett Ryan, "Mailer and the Diet of Reality," in *Norman Mailer's Later Fictions,* ed. Whalen-Bridge, 43.

15. Interview with C. Bigsby, BBC Radio 3, "Third Ear," 12 November 1991; interview with Barry Leeds, in *Enduring Vision of Norman Mailer,* 118.

16. Denis Donoghue, "Death on the Windy Dunes," *New York Times,* 29 July 1984.

17. See Barry Leeds's *Enduring Vision of Norman Mailer* for a detailed comparison of the two novels.

18. Scott Duguid, "From Egypt to Provincetown, by Trump Air," in *Norman Mailer's Later Fictions,* ed. Whalen-Bridge, 19.

19. *Conversations with Norman Mailer,* 43.

20. Barry Leeds, by contrast, argues that Mailer "is able to evoke even more fully than he did in his novel the bleakness of his Provincetown winter" and the "excesses of the murder mystery plot" are "ameliorated to some degree by a pervasive tone of black humor" (*Enduring Vision of Norman Mailer,* 90).

21. Interview with Michael Glenday, 21 October 1991, cited in Glenday's *Norman Mailer.*

22. In a similar vein, after also having an affair with Dix Butler, CIA informant Chevi claims he "lost the connection to my manhood" (1117).

23. Mailer, *Advertisements for Myself,* 211.

24. Marina Rosenthal, "Spiritual Wickedness in High Places: Trauma, Violence, and Betrayal in *Harlot's Ghost,*" *Mailer Review* 7 (2013): 252.

25. David Anshen, "A New Politics of Form in *Harlot's Ghost,*" *Mailer Review* 2 (2008): 455, 459.

26. Both Jeffrey Partridge and Meshy Bernstein have noted that Mailer's Jesus embodies some of the themes and theologies Mailer himself has reflected upon over the years. In "A Jewish Reading of Norman Mailer's *The Gospel According to the Son,*" Bernstein calls Mailer's Jesus "a natural evolution from Mailer's early work," noting that this fictionalized Jesus "has been transformed in a way that makes him share many of the ideas of Mailer's earlier characters and certainly their theology" (in *Norman Mailer's Later Fictions,* ed. Whalen-Bridge, 80).

27. Michiko Kakutani, "*Gospel According to the Son:* Mailer's Perception of Jesus," *New York Times,* 14 April 1997.

Chapter 7—Concluding with Questions

1. Mailer, *The Big Empty,* 97–98.

2. "Mailer Opus," rpt. in Mailer, *Spooky Art,* 62.

3. Jeffrey Partridge, "Augustinian Evil in *The Gospel According to the Son* and *The Castle in the Forest*: A Case for Non-Dualism," in *Norman Mailer's Later Fictions,* ed. Whalen-Bridge (95).

4. Denise Levertov, "During the Eichmann Trial: i. When We Look Up." *Selected Poems*, edited by Paul A. Lacey. New York: New Directions, 2002. Page 27.

5. In addition to Partridge, Paul J. Griffiths also says that Mailer's depiction of evil is "decisively antidualist, the very reverse of Manichaean" ("Diabolical Conception," *Commonweal* 134, no. 9 [4 May 2007]: 24–26).

6. "Twelfth Round," interview with Robert Begiebing, 1983, rpt. in Mailer, *Spooky Art,* 162.

BIBLIOGRAPHY

Primary Sources

FICTION AND NONFICTION

The Naked and the Dead. N.Y.: Rinehart, 1948.
Barbary Shore. N.Y.: Rinehart, 1951.
The Deer Park. N.Y.: Putnam's 1955.
Deaths for the Ladies (and Other Disasters). N.Y.: Putnam's, 1962.
An American Dream. N.Y.: Dial P, 1965.
Why Are We in Vietnam? N.Y.: Putnam's, 1967.
The Armies of the Night. N.Y.: New American Library, 1968.
Miami and the Siege of Chicago. N.Y.: World Publishing, 1968.
Of a Fire on the Moon. Boston: Little, Brown & Co., 1971.
The Prisoner of Sex. Boston: Little, Brown & Co., 1971.
St. George and the Godfather. N.Y.: New American Library, 1972.
Marilyn. N.Y.: Grosset & Dunlap, 1973.
The Faith of Graffiti. With John Naar. N.Y.: Praeger, 1974.
The Fight. Boston: Little Brown & Co., 1975.
Genius and Lust. N.Y.: Grove, 1976.
The Executioner's Song. Little Brown & Co., 1979.
Of Women and Their Elegance. N.Y.: Simon & Schuster, 1980.
Ancient Evenings. Boston: Little, Brown, & Co., 1983.
Tough Guys Don't Dance. N.Y.: Random House, 1984.
Harlot's Ghost. N.Y.: Random House, 1991.
Oswald's Tale: An American Mystery. N.Y.: Random House, 1995.
Portrait of Picasso as a Young Man. N.Y.: Atlantic Monthly P, 1995.
The Gospel According to the Son. N.Y.: Random House, 1997.
The Spooky Art: Some Thoughts on Writing. N.Y.: Random House, 2003.
Why Are We at War? N.Y.: Random House, 2003.
The Big Empty. With John Buffalo Mailer. N.Y.: Nation Books, 2006.
The Castle in the Forest. N.Y.: Random House, 2007.
On God: An Uncommon Conversation. With Michael Lennon. N.Y.: Random House, 2007.

COLLECTIONS AND COMPILATIONS

Advertisements for Myself. N.Y.: Putnam's, 1959.
The Presidential Papers. N.Y.: Putnam's, 1963.
Cannibals and Christians. N.Y.: Dial, 1966.

The Short Fiction of Norman Mailer. N.Y.: Dell, 1967.
The Long Patrol. Ed. Robert F. Lucid. N.Y.: World Publishing, 1971.
Existential Errands. Boston: Little, Brown, & Co., 1972.
Pieces and Pontifications. Boston: Little, Brown, & Co., 1982.
Conversations with Norman Mailer. Ed. J. Michael Lennon. Jackson: UP of Mississippi, 1986.
The Time of Our Time. N.Y.: Random House, 1998.
The Mind of an Outlaw. Ed. Phillip Sipiora. N.Y.: Random House, 2013.
Selected Letters of Norman Mailer. Ed. J. Michael Lennon. N.Y.: Random House, 2014.

Secondary Sources

BOOKS

Adams, Laura. *Existential Battles: The Growth of Norman Mailer.* Athens: Ohio UP, 1976.
———, ed. *Will the Real Norman Mailer Please Stand Up.* Port Washington, N.Y.: Kennikat P, 1974.
Begiebing, Robert. *Acts of Regeneration: Allegory and Archetype in the Works of Norman Mailer.* Columbia: U of Missouri P, 1980.
Bloom, Harold, ed. *Critical Views: Norman Mailer.* Broomall, Pa.: Chelsea House Publishers, 2003.
Boone, Joseph Allen. *The Homoerotics of Orientalism.* N.Y.: Columbia UP, 2014.
Braudy, Leo. ed. *Norman Mailer: A Collection of Critical Essays.* Englewood Cliffs, N.J.: Prentice Hall, 1972.
Bufithis, Philip H. *Norman Mailer.* N.Y.: Frederick Unger, 1978.
Fuchs, Daniel. *The Limits of Ferocity: Sexual Aggression and Modern Literary Rebellion.* Durham, N.C.: Duke UP, 2011.
Glenday, Michael K. *Norman Mailer.* N.Y.: St. Martins, 1995.
———. "From Monroe to Picasso: Norman Mailer and the Life Study." *Mailer Review* 2 (Fall 2008): 348–63.
Gordon, Andrew. *An American Dreamer: A Psychoanalytic Study of the Fiction of Norman Mailer.* Cranbury, N.J.: Associated U Presses, 1980.
Kaufmann, Donald L. *Norman Mailer: The Countdown (The First Twenty Years).* Carbondale: Southern Illinois UP, 1969.
Leeds, Barry H. *The Structured Vision of Norman Mailer.* N.Y.: New York UP, 1969.
———. *The Enduring Vision of Norman Mailer.* Bainbridge Island, Wash.: Pleasure Boat Studio, 2002.
Leigh, Nigel. *Radical Fictions and the Novels of Norman Mailer.* N.Y.: St. Martin's P, 1990.
Lennon, J. Michael, ed. *Critical Essays on Norman Mailer.* Boston: G. K. Hall & Co., 1986.
———, and Donna Pedro Lennon. *Norman Mailer: Works and Days.* Shavertown, Pa.: Sligo P, 2000.
Lucid, Robert F., ed. *Norman Mailer: The Man and His Work.* Boston: Little, Brown & Co, 1971.
McKinley, Maggie. *Masculinity and the Paradox of Violence in American Fiction, 1950–75.* N.Y.: Bloomsbury, 2015.
Merrill, Robert. *Norman Mailer.* Boston: Twayne Publishing, 1978.
Millett, Kate. *Sexual Politics.* Garden City, N.Y.: Doubleday, 1970.

Poirier, Richard. *Norman Mailer.* N.Y.: Viking P, 1972.

Rosenberg, Warren. *Legacy of Rage: Jewish Masculinity, Violence, and Culture.* Amherst: U of Massachusetts P, 2001.

Schultz, Kevin M. *Buckley and Mailer: The Difficult Friendship That Shaped the Sixties.* N.Y.: W. W. Norton & Co., 2015.

Solotaroff, Robert. *Down Mailer's Way.* Urbana: U of Illinois P, 1974.

Wenke, Joseph. *Mailer's America.* Hanover, N.H.: UP of New England, 1987.

Whalen-Bridge, John, ed. *Norman Mailer's Later Fictions:* Ancient Evenings *through* Castle in the Forest. N.Y.: Palgrave Macmillan, 2010.

Wilson, Andrew. *Norman Mailer: An American Aesthetic.* N.Y.: Peter Lang, 2008.

BIOGRAPHIES

Dearborn, Mary V. *Mailer: A Biography.* N.Y.: Houghton Mifflin, 1999.

Lennon, J. Michael. *Norman Mailer: A Double Life.* N.Y.: Simon & Schuster, 2014.

Manso, Peter. *Mailer: His Life and Times.* N.Y.: Simon & Schuster, 1985.

Mills, Hillary. *Mailer: A Biography.* N.Y.: Empire Books, 1982.

Rollyson, Carl. *The Lives of Norman Mailer: A Biography.* N.Y.: Paragon House, 1991.

ARTICLES

Anshen, David. "The Prescience of Mailer's Marxism: Socialism or Barbary Shore." *Mailer Review* 6 (2012): 246–66.

Baldwin, James. "The Black Boy Looks at the White Boy." 1961. *James Baldwin: Collected Essays.* Ed. Toni Morrison. N.Y.: Library of America, 1998.

Batchelor, Bob. "Visions of the American Dream: F. Scott Fitzgerald, Bob Dylan, and Norman Mailer Probe the Heart of the National Idea." *Mailer Review* 7 (2013): 74–89.

Bernstein, Mashey. "Jewish Values in the Fiction of Norman Mailer." *Mailer Review* 2 (2008): 376–84.

Cappell, Ezra. "Hemingway's Jewish Progeny: Roth and Goldstein in *The Naked and the Dead.*" *Mailer Review* 4 (2010): 208–28.

Chaiken, Michael. "The Master's Mercurial Mistress: How Norman Mailer Courted Chaos 24 Frames per Second." *Film Comment* 43, no. 4 (July–August 2007): 36–42.

———. "Author, Auteur: A Conversation with Norman Mailer." *Mailer Review* 2 (2008): 407–20.

Cohen, Sara Jo. "Making Masculinity and Unmaking Jewishness: Norman Mailer's Voice in *Wild 90* and *Beyond the Law.*" *Mailer Review* 5 (2011): 183–98.

Decter, Midge. "Mailer's Campaign." *Commentary,* 1 February 1964, 83–84.

Edmundson, Mark. "Romantic Self-Creations: Mailer and Gilmore in *The Executioner's Song.*" *Contemporary Literature* 31, no. 4 (Winter 1990): 434–47.

Fried, Ronald K. "Mailer's Boxing Journalism." *Mailer Review* 7 (2013): 222–30.

Fulgham, Richard Lee. "The Wise Blood of Norman Mailer: An Interpretation and Defense of *Why Are We in Vietnam?*" *Mailer Review* 2 (2008): 337–47.

Greer, Germaine. "My Mailer Problem." *Esquire,* September 1971. Rpt. in *The Madwoman's Underclothes: Essays and Occasional Writings.* N.Y.: Atlantic Monthly P, 1986.

Mosser, Jason. "Genre Bending in *The Armies of the Night.*" *Mailer Review* 3 (2009): 307–21.

Olshaker, Mark. "The Crime of His Time." *Mailer Review* 3 (2009): 90–105.

Podhoretz, Norman. "Norman Mailer: The Embattled Vision." *Partisan Review* 26 (Summer 1959): 371–91. Rpt. as Introduction to *Barbary Shore.*

Trilling, Diana. "The Radical Moralism of Norman Mailer." *Claremont Essays.* N.Y.: Harcourt Brace, 1962.

Waldron, Randall H. "The Naked, the Dead, and the Machine: A New Look at Norman Mailer's First Novel." *PMLA* 87, no. 2 (March 1972): 271–77.

Wilson, Raymond J. "Control and Freedom in *The Naked and the Dead.*" *Texas Studies in Literature and Language* 28 (1986): 164–81.

INDEX